Ronaldo Lasakoswitsck

The Pedagogical Coordinator: from legislation to action

Ronaldo Lasakoswitsck

The Pedagogical Coordinator: from legislation to action

Duties and Practices

ScienciaScripts

Imprint

Cover image: www.ingimage.com

This book is a translation from the original published under ISBN 978-3-330-76135-3.

Publisher:
Sciencia Scripts
is a trademark of
Dodo Books Indian Ocean Ltd. and OmniScriptum S.R.L publishing group

120 High Road, East Finchley, London, N2 9ED, United Kingdom
Str. Armeneasca 28/1, office 1, Chisinau MD-2012, Republic of Moldova, Europe
Printed at: see last page
ISBN: 978-620-8-36328-4

The learned man is a discoverer of facts that already exist - but the wise man is a creator of values that don't exist and that he makes exist.

Albert Einstein

SUMMARY

The increase in the number of studies on pedagogical coordination in recent years reveals a certain consensus on the importance of the role of the Teacher Coordinator in schools. It also awakens the need to understand their attributions and practices in their day-to-day work, as well as underpinning the principles for their actions. Current researchers are concerned about the Teacher Coordinator in terms of issues related to educational pedagogical processes, transformations in teaching pedagogical conditions and teacher training. Inserted in a scenario marked by the presence of plural and diverse groups, such as teachers, students, the community and other education professionals, it becomes essential to define what the real attributions of the position are, the professional tasks and priorities that must be carried out in the day-to-day running of the school, so that their performance is effective. This study therefore focuses on the Teacher Coordinator in public education, taking as its object the Brazilian educational systems and, more specifically, the state primary and secondary schools in the city of Mauá in the state of São Paulo. The methodological design was defined as descriptive, adopting the qualitative method to collect and analyse the data. To this end, through a literature review, the research analysed the laws that define and guide the role and performance of the teacher coordinator. The study was then carried out in Mauá, SP, by means of document analysis, non-participant observation and in-depth interviews. The social subjects of the research were chosen intentionally, forming a group of eleven Teacher Coordinators. They answered a structured questionnaire with dichotomous questions about their knowledge of the legislation that guides the performance and execution of their actions in everyday school life. Later, during a working week, the respondents filled in a diary revealing the main tasks they carry out every hour during their working day. Using the triangulation technique and the content analysis technique advocated by Bardin (1971), it was possible to observe the existence of differences between the definitions supported by legislation for the performance of the Teacher Coordinator and the attributions and actions revealed on a daily basis.

Keywords: Coordinating teacher. Legislation. Performance. Duties. Action in everyday school life.

SUMMARY

PRESENTATION

Of the almost thirty years I worked as an educator in São Paulo, sixteen years I worked as a pedagogical coordinator. This brought me closer to the administrative area and, in practice, I was able to gather experience in the performance of this role. Over time, I realised the need to study and research in order to propose new ways and solutions to the day-to-day action I was presented with every day. And I realised more and more how important the role of the pedagogical coordinator was. In this scenario, in Brazilian primary and secondary schools, the teacher coordinator is situated in the middle of a triad: the headteacher, teachers and pupils, which sometimes expands into other subjects: the headteacher's office and those responsible for the pupils. They often become the lightning rod for professional relationships in the school environment.

The specific courses I have taken during my professional life, in pedagogical coordination, post-graduate studies in people management, and the professional master's degree in educational management and practices, which I am now completing, have become sources of answers to support my experience and provide the knowledge to carry out and develop studies that seek to answer the questions about the duties of the teacher coordinator. The more I delve into the relationships and responsibilities of this fundamental part of school life, the more I realise the need to find other ways to contribute to the successful execution of their work. In this way, this research report is based on a study of the coordinating teacher, from the point of view of what is defined and supported by the legislation in force in Brazil and in the state of São Paulo, and on the review and observation of the study context, as well as on the understanding of the actors in the action, the coordinating teachers of the State Primary and Secondary Schools. The aim of this scientific research is to contribute to the theme of contemporary educational management and to the Line of Research and Intervention in Educational Management (LIPIGES) at the University of Nove de Julho (UNINOVE), as well as to broaden the understanding of the environment of the practice of action, proposing the intervention that may be appropriate for the continuous improvement of the resources and means put at the service of the educational systems that are the object of study here.

CHAPTER 1

INTRODUCTION

The subject of this research, due to changes in the educational reforms of the state of São Paulo's educational legislation, has had various nomenclatures associated with him: Student Inspector, Pedagogical Assistant, Educational Supervisor, School Supervisor, Pedagogical Coordinator, Pedagogical Teacher Coordinator, Teacher Coordinator, and Pedagogical Management Support Teacher Coordinator. In this work, the nomenclature of the official text of Resolution SE 88/2007, which is still in force and regulates, is maintained, and because the research population is centred on the State Primary and Secondary Schools in the region of Mauá, São Paulo, which naturally follow that Resolution. Therefore, the research subject will be referred to as the Coordinating Teacher (CP) throughout this study.

The literature that draws attention to the importance of the role of the Teacher Coordinator in the school environment is significantly numerous. The increase in the number of studies on the subject of pedagogical coordination in recent years reveals a certain consensus on the growing importance of this professional in Brazilian schools. Current researchers are focussing on issues related to the articulation and pedagogical processes of education, transformations in the pedagogical conditions of teaching and teacher training. It is believed that these studies collaborate directly with the contemporary problem of understanding their role, functions, attributions and, consequently, their professional identity (LAURINDA, 2012, 2011; ALMEIDA, 2012, 2011; PLACCO, 2012, 2011, 2010; SOUZA, 2013, 2010; DOMINGUES, 2011, 2009; FERNANDES, 2012, 2011, 2009, 2007, 2004; BRUNO, 2010; CHRISTOV, 2010).

They are known as dialogue agents who must be attentive to the transformations of the institution's participants, promoting reflections on school relations and the transformation of pedagogical practice. In carrying out the multiple activities that characterise his role, he establishes various partnerships through interpersonal relationships. It is necessary for educational action to be planned and articulated with school subjects and the pedagogical coordinator presents himself as a mediator of interactive forms of work, in moments of study, propositions, reflections and actions. However, for this to happen efficiently, it is necessary for educational action to be planned and shared between the Teacher Coordinator and all the other social subjects that coexist in the school system: teacher, headmaster, parents and guardians.

The authors Placco, Almeida and Souza (2010) confirm some of the main duties of the Teacher Coordinator:

> [...] the coordinator's attributions, in terms of the training dimension, are based on: promoting the articulation of the school team to draw up the school's political-pedagogical project; mediating interpersonal relationships; planning, organising and conducting pedagogical meetings; dealing with the power relations that are unleashed in the school; carrying out their practice taking into account the diversity of teachers and schools; making written records as a way of sustaining the authorship of their role in the school. In order to do this, specific knowledge is required, in addition to teaching knowledge, although anchored in it, which points to the need for new learning, both for the adult teacher and the adult coordinator.

These actions also refer to the training, articulating and transforming dimension of the PC, because the school is the space for cognitive construction, the unveiling of cultures and integration. That's why it's important that their professional practice always includes values and attitudes relating to the practice of justice, tolerance and democracy. For this to be validated, Article 6, paragraph 1 must be observed, which states that the pedagogical coordinator must "coordinate the preparation, development, monitoring and evaluation of the pedagogical proposal, together with teachers and other school unit managers, in line with the principles of participatory democratic management and curricular provisions, as well as the objectives and goals to be achieved". (SE 3, 18/01/2013)

It is important that CPs see themselves as an indissoluble part of the school institution, and this presupposes that they draw up their work plan in accordance with the pedagogical political project and the general guidelines for their professional practice, and that it is contained in an environment that provides them with the tools to carry out their duties.

In this sense, and in accordance with the current educational reality, giving due importance to the role and profile of the CP is a relevant aspect of this research. To this end, the state primary and secondary school is the research site, and the CPs are the research subjects. Thus, considering the problem and the assumptions raised, the following objectives will guide the work:

In the 1970s, the position of Coordinating Teacher was created and its strategic function was to converge relations between the teaching staff, students and school management. The PC's role was to involve the school's educators, teachers and staff in the processes of analysing and diagnosing the school's reality, as well as planning and proposing projects to meet the diagnosed needs and the school's objectives (PLACCO, 2010).

Even with the passing of the years and changes in the law, the main objective of his job is to guarantee a healthy and successful learning process for the students on the course he works on. To this end, they carry out various tasks on a daily basis: bureaucratic tasks, dealing with students and parents, looking after and planning the entire educational process of the course, as well as emergencies and unforeseen events (VIEIRA, 2010, p. 83).

This justifies the need to understand the importance and value the role of this actor in school management. Regardless of conflicts, functions, teaching modalities or attributions, it can be concluded that the position of Coordinating Teacher also has an important managerial content in school administration and, therefore, must have this competence developed, generating quality for the whole process.

Within the various state and municipal education systems, the search for an identity and the definition of the Teacher Coordinator's occupational profile is a major challenge. This is because, despite the fact that the texts published in the law clearly define what their duties and tasks should be, there is still no definite consensus on the nomenclatures that are attributed to them. Today, the term Teacher Coordinator (PC) is used at state level, while at municipal level it is Pedagogical Coordinator (CP). In some regions of Brazil, terms such as Pedagogue and Pedagogical Supervisor may also appear.

However, notwithstanding the vagueness of the nomenclature, it can be said that among all the activities carried out, the Teacher Coordinator interacts mainly and directly with the teachers and other managers in the school environment, and it is up to them to observe their own relational behaviours that focus on the development of teaching work in the classroom and its proper articulation with the school's planning and management.

In order to better fulfil this role, it is necessary to distinguish and value communication and information management processes and spaces. In a scenario marked by the presence of plural and diverse groups, such as teachers, students, the community and other education professionals, understanding that the school is a multicultural institution par excellence is extremely important. The Coordinating Teacher is the interlocutor for building democratic interpersonal relationships, demanding respect for the ethical principle of valuing both the person and the education professional, taking into account cultural diversity and understanding pedagogical concepts, as well as understanding the process of building the school's institutional identity.

By promoting the articulation of the school team around the Pedagogical Political Project (PPP), coordinating discussions and analysing its development in teaching plans, course plans and lesson plans, the pedagogical coordinator takes on a central role in school planning. The articulation around the PPP will allow different school subjects to move in the direction of the objectives and goals established by the school collective. In this process, the pedagogical coordinator also learns from the reflective considerations and feedback of the other school players, and the school becomes a learning organisation.

For Freire (1996), teaching does not exist without learning and vice versa, and it was through social learning that men and women historically discovered that it was possible to teach.

According to Freire (1982), the coordinator is an educator and, as such, must be attentive to the pedagogical nature of learning relationships within the school. He didn't believe in quick and immediate formulas: "We don't believe in summer training courses, we want programmes to discuss practice, in ongoing training groups, which unearth theory from within practice, this requires competence on the part of those who coordinate". (SALVADOR, 2002)

The actions of the Teacher Coordinator, in the exercise of his function, need to consider that learning is a collective construction, which is why he needs to create, among the teachers, a space for the re-signification of their practices, in order to recover autonomy over their work without, however, distancing himself from the collective work of the school.

They must not lose sight of their role in the education of pupils and teachers, in the school's collective, thus reviewing their practices and building new ones.

This raises the research question that will guide this investigation:

To what extent do the functions and attributions of the Teacher Coordinator correspond to what is established in the legislation in force in the state of São Paulo and, more specifically, in the State Public Network of the city of Mauá?

1.1 GENERAL OBJECTIVE

With this guiding perspective, the general objective is to:

To analyse the performance of the Teacher Coordinator in the State Public Network of the city of Mauá, in the state of São Paulo, in their daily lives, in terms of their functions and attributions, established by legislation.

1.2 SPECIFIC OBJECTIVES

In turn, the specific objectives focus on:

- Analysing the effectiveness and efficiency of the activities carried out by the Coordinating Teacher in relation to the duties set out in the legislation;

- Identify the functions and attributions of the Teacher Coordinator in the performance and execution of tasks, in the act of action;

- Comparing the legislation in force and the Teacher Coordinator's praxis in the act of action;

- To analyse which functions and attributions the Teacher Coordinator feels are due to their effective performance in the school;

- Propose guidelines for the functions and attributions of the Teacher Coordinator, taking into account current legislation, school praxis and the understanding of due performance in the act of action, seeking to make the role of this Teacher Coordinator legitimate, as a manager with the teachers in the school.

CHAPTER 2

COORDINATING TEACHER: MANAGER OF WHAT?

Studies on the role of the pedagogical manager in school organisations have spread throughout scientific literature all over the world, and exponentially. Placco, Almeida and Souza (2011) briefly show in O Coordenador Pedagógico (CP) e a formação de professores: intenções, tensões e contradições that some studies carried out in Canada and France point to pedagogical coordination as vital for the school context. Also in Chile, Nicaragua, Mozambique, Portugal and Canada (Ontario), successful experiences always indicate the presence of a professional who articulates training in the school. (PLACCO; ALMEIDA; SOUZA, 2011, p. 236)

> [...] in France or Canada, the tasks of this professional, called a pedagogical counsellor, revolve around the three axes that characterise the role of the PC in Brazil - trainer, articulator and transformer. It is also evident that their areas of activity, functions, attributions and, above all, the role of coordinator reveal that the educational systems in these countries recognise the need for a professional in school education to mediate educational processes. (PLACCO; ALMEIDA; SOUZA, 2011, p. 231-232)

Regardless of the type of organisation, whether it is in the first, second or third sector, management requires people who are able to carry out the different managerial functions, from basic planning, organisation, coordination, control and evaluation studies to the more specific ones that lead to decision making, in modern administration, and within a broader understanding of the institution's philosophy and mission. It can be seen from the theoretical framework and the movement of new legislation that public organisations have been looking for alternatives that make it possible to apply the modern administration model, while respecting the specific contexts and ideologies that permeate understandings, and which are present in each era. As public organisations are essentially focused on providing services in their various sectors, adopting a management approach focused on quality in the provision of these services is one of the main points of convergence for dealing with the challenges of globalisation and the digital information age, which cannot be ignored, and which influence these organisations as well as economic, social, technological and political aspects, among others.

Public organisations that provide education services include primary and secondary schools. As an organisation, it is also seeking to manage with modernity and with a focus on educational quality. However, according to Russo (2004, p. 26-27)

> Given all the threats and difficulties to consolidating the changes that are on the horizon, especially the obstacles that come from the resistance movement of conservative forces, a theory that sheds light on the transition is crucial to ensuring a conscious transformation of reality. Hence the importance we attach in this text to the theoretical-paradigmatic question of educational administration, identifying a challenge in it. [...] it will be necessary to rethink the school that is there, insofar as it has historically served the dominant interests not only as an instrument of domestication, resulting in poor results, but also because it has been guided by conservative theoretical thinking that reveals to education the almost exclusive role of reproducing the labour force.

This confirms the tendency of school organisation practices to be rooted in deeper issues, showing that "The challenges of educational administration have their origins before the current situation and politics in Brazil and worldwide: they are structural challenges, both of a theoretical and practical nature, that education faces in capitalism". (RUSSO, 2004, p. 27)

Studies by authors such as Paro (1991) and Russo (1995) reveal that the school organisation is still based on an administration based on the General Theory of Administration (TGA), both in the expression of its way of thinking and in the formulation of its practices. According to Russo (2011),

> The issue has received attention from educational administration scholars and there is still no consensus on it. Although critical school administration proposals have been developed over the last three decades, with a view to transforming education, there is still a persistent and dominant conservative practice, supported by concepts that are anchored in the foundations of business administration, so much to the liking of neoliberal policies. (RUSSO, 2011, 497-498)

However, it should be noted that, even with this neoliberal bias, since the late 1980s the role of the public school administrator has been revised, undergoing changes, the impacts of which have not yet been fully clarified.

With regard to the Coordinating Teacher in public schools, who can be seen as a school manager, the trajectory of his problem reveals that, specifically in São Paulo, the position of CP in the state public network has already changed a few times, through various designations, over time, and consequently its functions have ended up being diverted and associated with its main functions. Much of this can be credited to the evolution of a position that in the past was known as School Inspector, and whose main function was only to control the presence of students and teachers at school.

From the outset, before the Pedagogical Coordinator position was actually created[1] , there was no definition of a career, because according to Roman (2001, p.20), "Inspectors were not even paid at this time, nor did they follow any defined work organisation. The professional status of this position only came about with the 1920 reform, and even then, they were not part of the school staff. The scenario began *to* change twenty-two years later when "the supervisory function expressed in terms of coordination, guidance or pedagogical assistance appears in the legislation from 1942 onwards." (ROMAN, 2001). It should be noted that the pedagogical function began to be included in the purely administrative position, even though the title of Pupil Inspector was not changed, and its support functions for teachers were not being carried out directly in the school units. According to Roman (2001), it wasn't until the title was changed to Educational Advisor that "around 1945" this professional became an integral part of the school staff.

Around 1957, some primary school teachers were sent to the United States of America to be trained and to teach supervisor training courses, which would be distributed throughout Brazil. (GARCIA, 1995) The course covered some areas of knowledge that could be understood as the duties of the position, such as: planning, rational organisation of pedagogical actions, separation between the concept and execution of the work, specialisation of functions, control of the process and bureaucratisation. All of these attributions, in line with the restructuring of the entire educational system, were regulated in the Law of Guidelines and Bases (LDB), Law 4024 of 1961, which created a qualification for the position of supervisor, with one caveat, because it was only in 1974, with the extinction of the position of pupil inspector, that the position of teaching supervisor was circumscribed in the first LDB, in articles 62 to 65 of chapter 8:

> Art. 62: The education counsellor will be trained in special courses that meet the conditions of the level of the type of teaching and the social environment for which they are intended.
>
> Art. 63: In philosophy faculties, a special course will be created for the training of high school education counsellors, to which graduates in pedagogy, philosophy, psychology or social sciences will have access, as well as graduates in Physical Education from the Higher Schools of Physical Education and federal education inspectors, all with at least three years of teaching experience.
>
> Art. 64: Primary school guidance counsellors will be trained at educational institutes in a special course to which graduates of normal high schools and educational institutes will have access, with a minimum of three years' training in primary teaching.

[1] Nomenclature that appears in Complementary Law 114 of 1974, art. 12 to 14.

> Art. 65: The inspector of education, chosen through a public examination for qualifications and vetted tests , must have technical and pedagogical knowledge.
> demonstrated preferably in the exercise of teaching functions as a school administration assistant or in the direction of an educational establishment.

From this period onwards, CFE Opinion No 252/69 determined that the training of school supervisors would take place in a higher education pedagogy course. The qualification in School Supervision would allow the professional to work in technical-administrative bodies and in the school unit, while the Pedagogical Coordinator would take on this title when exercising the position in schools.

From 1969 onwards, bodies responsible for structuring and providing pedagogical support to state schools were created, and the role of "Pedagogical Assistant" was expanded based on State Law 7376 of 31 October 1962. According to Roman (2001, p.14):

> From 1963 to 1969, central bodies were created that were responsible for structuring technical pedagogical support for state schools. Despite the fact that the administrative restructuring of the Department of Education that took place in 1969 had, due to a lack of investment and personnel, scrapped some of these bodies, the role of Pedagogical Assistant was expanded in 1970, and implemented in the Pluricurricular or Multipurpose Gymnasiums, the Gymnasium School Groups and the schools that adopted the didactic-administrative action plan along the lines of renewed education, according to Article 4 of the Resolution of 30/07/70, published in the D.O.E. São Paulo, of 31/07/70.

An example of the confusion of forces outside the school, which are manifested through laws, is the fact that the positions (Pedagogical Coordinator, Pedagogical Supervisor and Pedagogical Adviser) ended up differentiating themselves and finding the physical location for their execution only recently - namely, according to Andreucci (1999), "the use of the name Pedagogical Coordinator for the professional who performs the supervisory function in the school unit only appears in the law in 1976" initially defined by Decrees No. 1 and No. 2.[0]

5.586 of 1975 and No. 7709 of 1976, spacing out, or diverging from the point of view of Garcia (1999) who says that the fact only occurred in the Statute of the State Magisterium in 1974, in Complementary Law 114, which indicates in Articles 12 to 14:

> Article 12 - Each school will have one (1) Pedagogical Coordinator.
> Sole Paragraph - The Pedagogical Coordinator will be appointed in

> accordance with the regulations and must be a teacher who has:
> 1. Higher education course corresponding to a full degree in Pedagogy;
> 2. Preferably with a specific qualification in School Supervision;
> 3. At least 5 (five) years of effective teaching in the teaching career.
> Article 13 - There may be teacher-coordinators for areas of the Full Curriculum, in accordance with the scope and basic organisation of the school, as provided for in the school regulations.
> Sole Paragraph - The appointment to the role of Teacher-Coordinator must fall to a teacher who has:
> 1. Undergraduate degree corresponding to a full honours degree in at least one of the subjects in the area in which they are to work:
> 2. At least 3 (three) years of effective teaching in the teaching career.
> Article 14 - The number of Assistant Headteacher, Pedagogical Coordinator and Teacher Coordinator positions will be fixed by decree in accordance with the basic organisation of the school.

However, researchers agree that the Pedagogical Coordinator is the professional who works with schools, while the School Supervisor works with content and study methods, and finally, the Guidance Counsellor works with students.

Observing the conflicts and deviations of functions, considering the changes in the nomenclature of functions over time, the question unfolds about the functions and delimitations of the research subject's position. In addition, according to Gatti, Bernardes and Mello (1974), one of the main functions of the Pedagogical Assistant is to be an agent of innovation, prepared to face resistance to change, obstacles and authoritarianism. He goes on to say that this professional does not have a teaching or administrative role, but is characterised by: a) integrating the school environment; b) [dealing with] ...planning, the curriculum, the integration of programmes, and evaluation and execution procedures...; c) interaction with all the elements involved in the school. For this reason, the authors point out that, from that moment on, the diversion of functions and the ambiguity of attributions were constant hallmarks of the Pedagogical Assistant's work.

The definition of the role of Teacher Coordinator is still ambiguous and sometimes confusing. Scientific articles show that the role is changed at the whim of internal and external political forces, depending on the social and historical moment. It is understood that, in this scenario, there are internal and external political forces. Those who hold senior positions within the school where the Coordinating Teacher is to fulfil his/her role are often unaware of the CP's legal duties and functions, and even the teacher who takes on this role is unaware of this new position. As a result, they receive and take on an overload of activities that don't belong to their main function, which is to provide ongoing training for teachers. This is evident in the opening text of SE Resolution 88/2007, which provides for the bonus position of Teacher Coordinator, when it refers to the objectives:

> - Expanding students' knowledge and expertise, raising the level of academic performance shown by external and internal assessment instruments;
>
> - Intervene in teaching practice, encouraging teachers to diversify learning opportunities, with a view to overcoming the difficulties detected in students;
>
> - Promote the improvement and professional development of designated teachers, with a view to making their work more effective and better. (SE No. 88/2007)

SE Resolution 88/2007, still in the 1980s, set out the duties of the coordinating teacher, defining him as one of the "structural pillars" of quality education, and that he should act as a manager who implements public policies.

This problem is reflected in the field of Educational Management, since this lack of professional identity and security in carrying out the work means that the CP, despite knowing that he is very important to the educational process, finds himself bogged down in unfocused tasks and carrying out tasks that contribute little to educational procedures. In fact, the embarrassment of tasks, coupled with the lack of communication between peers, effective feedback, and the exercise of purely bureaucratic emergency tasks, make it difficult and distance them from the process of building this identity.

It is therefore assumed, based on the discourse of Domingues (2009), that the professional profile of the Teacher Coordinator is marked by a scenario of changing political and educational values, which results in instability, a weakening of social representation, and the de-characterisation of their actions in the professional sphere. It can also be assumed that the role and duties of this coordinator are complex. The legislation that regulates this matter is at federal, state and municipal level. In this way, it is not always clear what these teaching professionals are responsible for, which can also lead to a lack of clarification about their duties in the position. It can also be assumed, based on the work of the Victor Civita Foundation (FCV) and the Carlos Chagas Foundation (FCC), published in the Nova Escola magazine, special edition of June/July 2011, and the thesis by Isaneida Domingues (2009), entitled O coordenador pedagógico e o desafio da formação contínua do docente na escola (The pedagogical coordinator and the challenge of continuous teacher training at school), that recently investigated situations show that the work of the pedagogical coordinator, according to the focus of the research, is a multidetermined 'know-how', resulting from factors such as personal development, institutional organisation and public policies. In addition, they showed the fragility of the initial training of the Teacher Coordinator and the ongoing training offered. They also show that the PC needs time to build a formative identity so that they can establish a leadership facet based on an indeterminate amount of time for their reflective and critical training.

So, to summarise, it can be said that, despite almost four decades having passed since the position was distinguished and defined, at least in its title, this professional still has undefined managerial situations. With the exception of the text of SE Resolution No. 1/2013, which presents attributes based on managerial characteristics, there is still no real clarity when it comes to the attributions and responsibilities of this professional. Generally speaking, if you look quickly at academic papers on the subject, it's clear that the functions and role of the pedagogical coordinator as a manager are not well understood, "being able to plan, monitor and evaluate the teaching and learning processes, as well as the performance of managers, teachers and students". (SE 3/2007)

Authors investigating the functions and duties of the Coordinating Teacher, such as Fernandes (2011 and 2009), Waldmann and Schneltzler (2007), Domingues (2009), Magalhães (2011), contribute to analysing the main resolutions on the role of the CP, indicating that the attributions and functions were appropriated by the educational reforms. These reforms distorted the objectives and ways of working of the CP, giving it a role closer to centralised administrative power than to school organisations and subjects in the pedagogical sphere. This has left or split the emphasis on continuing teacher training, which aims to manage the roles, places and conflicts experienced by teachers.

In the context of state schools in the state of São Paulo, the professional who joins this cadre is usually a teacher with a degree in any subject, which is not a specific qualification for the position. The title, at the moment, is Teacher Pedagogical Coordinator (PCP).

> The expansion of the PCP function to almost all schools in the state education network was guaranteed in the midst of the educational reforms through the publication of SE Resolution No. 28 of 4 April 1996, which provided details on the selection process for appointing a teacher to carry out the pedagogical coordination function. [...] The great novelty of this resolution was that, as well as guaranteeing in practice what had already been announced legally, it allowed any teacher with more than three years' experience in the São Paulo teaching profession to hold the position of PCP, regardless of their initial training, which meant that they did not need to have a degree in Pedagogy with a qualification in School Supervision, nor did they need to accumulate

> extensive professional experience. In this way, the Department of Education made it possible for teachers with no specific qualification and little teaching experience to take on the task of pedagogical coordination. Thus, the position would not be occupied by an "expert" in education, a specialist, but by a peer, a person who would have to occupy a position that presupposes constant coexistence with the difficulties and dilemmas present in the daily lives of public school teachers. (FERNANDES, 2007, p. 2)

It should be explained that in the current legislation, this is not a position but an occupational assignment that offers no status or guarantee of permanence, and that at any time or at the end of the term, the position can be removed in order to be replaced by another available professional. This situation no longer occurs at municipal level, since the professional is a CP, and in order to join the school, he or she must go through a selection process in accordance with Municipal Law 6235 of 28 August 1986. However, the same conflict can be seen for both professionals at both state and municipal levels. The teacher who takes on the position of pedagogical coordinator does not have the resources to carry out some important and essential tasks, such as guidance and support for the teachers in their school. Their daily tasks, conceived as routine, take over their diaries, involving them in a hundred 'hands-on' tasks, leaving behind the time for planning and intervening in the educational process.

It is worth noting the lack of consistency in the definition of positions and functions according to the São Paulo public school system, when Fernandes (2007, p. 14) states that:

> In the hierarchical structure of São Paulo's education network, there are positions and functions. Positions are filled by means of a public examination of tests and titles, regulated by public notices that allow the successful candidate to take up a position in the state civil service, guaranteeing job stability and incorporation into the staff of the Department of Education. The position is always a temporary occupation because it is not linked to a public competition for entry and promotion, so it is not legally foreseen as a position to be held for an indefinite period of time. Access to a position is through appointments, i.e. authorisations for an employee of the Department of Education to temporarily carry out activities provided for in the Teaching Statute.

He adds:

> We say that the role of pedagogical coordinator teacher was already legally provided for because an analysis of the legislation governing state schools allowed us to see that the Statute of the Magisterium from the 1970s (1974 and 1978) already provided for the role, although until the 1990s it only took place in specific experiments carried out by the State Education Department. (FERNANDES, p. 14)

Since there are declared conflicts and a lack of clarity about the role of the Coordinating

Teacher, although in contemporary times the concept of the CP is that of manager of the institution's Pedagogical Political Project, this professional is still seen and often maintains a posture of supervisor of the teacher's work and the student's behaviour. According to Ferreira (2007, p. 114), "No matter how much it is tried to be made up or argued, supervision continues to have the stigma of bureaucratic control that has characterised it since its origin, legitimised by resolution 02/71". According to Magalhães (2011), it thus retains "an attitude based on archaic education, in which the transfer of information and the control of pedagogical work are its main objectives".

Recently, according to Revista Nova Escola (2010, p.12), some actions have been shown to support the professional through definitions of the distribution of working hours, specifying that, in the public network, they should fulfil two thirds of their workload developing tasks of interaction with the students (§4, art.2). Presumably, the PC would make use of these two-thirds to show their relevance as the most developed pair able to encourage, organise and develop collective and individual education. It is known, however, from a survey carried out by Ibope, commissioned by the Victor Civita Foundation (FVC), of several state public school coordinators in 2010, that they are unaware of many issues pertaining to their work routine and the subjects that they should address and conduct during HTPC meetings (Hora de Trabalho Pedagógico Coletivo), now called ATPC (Aula de Trabalho Pedagógico Coletivo), seriously jeopardising the proposal for ongoing teacher training, and consequently the professional training of all.

According to the National Education Guidelines and Bases Law (LDB), the Teacher Coordinator's academic training takes place in two ways, either through a Pedagogy degree course, where their work should take place in Basic Education, or in postgraduate courses (LDB 9394/96, article 64). However, the LDB does not directly address the areas in which CP can work, but only makes it clear that the professional who undergoes one of the above training programmes must include training and a vision of administration, planning, inspection, supervision and educational guidance. Once again, there is a conflict when it comes to hiring this professional who hasn't necessarily travelled this previous path to occupy the position in question. Although evident in the research The Pedagogical Coordinator and Teacher Training: Intentions, Tensions and Contradictions, commissioned by the Victor Civita Foundation (FCV) from the Carlos Chagas Foundation (FCC), published in the Nova Escola magazine, special edition of June/July 2011, it can be seen that 55% of Coordinating Teachers are trained in Pedagogy, and that 70% have taken a postgraduate course, not proving that the latter percentage includes teachers from other degrees as well as Pedagogy graduates themselves, however, it can still be detected that only 4% of these professionals go on to more specialised courses (strictu senso). Allied to this discontinuity or inconsistency in training, these Teacher Coordinators have been in their jobs for an average of three and a half years.

Continuing the relationship between the roles of the Teacher Coordinator, according to Christov (2010), the essential role of the PC is undoubtedly associated with the process of in-service teacher training. This process has been called Continuing Education, both in official texts from municipal and state education departments and in recent literature on in-service training. Given this concept, it is clear that the CP is considered to be one of those responsible for the process of in-service training for teachers, in other words, for the Continuing Education of these professionals in everyday school life.

Recently published legislation SE No. 22 of 14/02/2012 and SE No. 3 of 18/01/2013, "considering that pedagogical coordination is one of the structural pillars of the current policy to improve teaching quality" (SE No. 22/2012), reinforces the professional profile and characteristics desired of this professional in order to bring them closer to school management. The explicit attributions in these Resolutions indicate a professional with managerial qualities and characteristics.

2.1 THE COORDINATING TEACHER IN CONTEXT

The school, perceived by some as an arena of conflict, can be understood, however, as an organisation where the management of resources and means must be put at the service of quality education, aiming for excellence, given that the whole process of institutional evaluation emanating from the federal and state governments is consolidated in PISA, SARESP and IDESP[2] . These instruments were created to measure performance in order to define and refine public policies, making it more effective to train young people to participate in active social life. The characteristics of the micro-political perspective are found at school: interests, conflict, power and negotiation (COSTA,

[2] PISA - *Programme for International Student Assessment.* The aim of PISA is to produce indicators that contribute to the discussion of the quality of education in the participating countries, in order to subsidise policies to improve basic education; SARESP - São Paulo School Performance Assessment System. Its purpose is to produce a diagnosis of the basic schooling situation in São Paulo's public education network, with the aim of guiding education managers in monitoring policies aimed at improving educational quality; IDESP - São Paulo State Education Development Index. This is a quality indicator that provides schools with a diagnosis of their quality, pointing out where they need to improve and signalling their progress year on year.

2003). In order to overcome the school's daily difficulties, there is a need for collective work, which in turn requires the presence and action of an organiser of the educational processes that take place there. This coordinator needs to work in different spaces and times, whether to develop curricular proposals or to attend to teachers, students and parents, in the various combinations that each school has.

It is in this context that the Coordinating Teacher appears to be in a privileged position, as he or she has "an articulating, training and transforming function" (ALMEIDA and PLACCO, 2010) and is therefore the professional mediator between the curriculum and the teachers. However, in the current panorama, he is also approaching the school administration as a management partner.

Given the importance of the Teacher Coordinator, the subject of this study, who is responsible for pedagogical quality and a partner in the school's administrative area, it is important to delve deeper into the characteristics and attributions that permeate their workplace in order to make them more focussed, obtaining better results and, consequently, achieving goals more effectively.

2.2 CURRENT UNDERSTANDING OF THE COORDINATING TEACHER AS SCHOOL MANAGER

In view of the above, it can be assumed that, on being hired to work as a pedagogical coordinator, the teacher or professional with pedagogical training in both higher education should proceed to act on the basis of the duties of the position. Once it is possible to focus on the job, and this professional can carry out the tasks efficiently and effectively, the benefits will be many. At first glance, the CP will be expected to work directly with students' learning problems, develop teaching materials, explore theories and foundations, orientate discipline problems, and work on issues of teacher and student motivation and performance.

The core of the Educational Management Research and Intervention Group (LIPIGES), linked to the Educational Management and Practices Programme (PROGEPE) and aligned with the Contemporary Educational Management research group (GRUGEC), aims to study and deepen the middle activity in education. The teacher coordinator is part of this process and is an integral part of the school environment, being an indissoluble part of educational management, both for execution and for pedagogical and administrative evaluation.

To make this a reality, actions are needed that support teamwork and management that prioritises teacher training, contributing to a quality administrative process. According to Chiavenato (1997, p.101), "it is no longer a question of managing people, but of managing with people. Organisations increasingly need proactive, responsible, dynamic, intelligent people with the skills to solve problems and make decisions". From this perspective, we must identify teachers' needs and work with them to find solutions that prioritise quality educational work.

This professional has to go beyond theoretical knowledge, because monitoring pedagogical work and stimulating teachers requires perception and sensitivity to identify the needs of students and teachers, and they have to keep up to date, seeking out sources of information and reflecting on their practice. According to Nóvoa (1992), "experience is neither formative nor productive. It is reflection on experience that can provoke the production of knowledge and training." With this in mind, it is also necessary to emphasise that the work must take place with everyone's collaboration, so the coordinator must be prepared for changes and always ready to motivate their team. One of their many duties is to monitor the work of the teaching staff, being responsible for the link between those involved in the educational community.

The issue of the relationship between the coordinator and the teacher is a crucial factor for democratic management, and in order for this to happen with well-formulated strategies, the coordinator must not lose focus.

Clarifying the current understanding of the PC, in the new SE Resolution No. 3 of 2013, which provides mechanisms to support the school's pedagogical management to implement the actions established by the Education - São Paulo Commitment Programme, it can be seen that the Coordinating Teacher is part of the school's management core, and should therefore develop the pedagogical management of the school units through actions and efforts. To this end, Article 5 of the Resolution sets out the attributes, competences and skills required of teachers in the role of Teacher Coordinator for Pedagogical Management Support:

- be able to plan, monitor and evaluate;
- have dynamism, a spirit of leadership and know how to relate to others;
- know how to work in a team;
- learn about conceptions of management practices and democratic and participatory

management;

- promote integration;

- have proactive attitudes;

- analysing external indices and indicators for evaluating the system and the school's performance, in order to make decisions;

- analysing internal indicators (SE No. 3, 18/01/2013)

These are points that focus on contemporary school management. It is vitally important for the Teacher Coordinator to approach these attributes outlined in the field of management. By carrying out their work in a focused and conscientious manner, the PC will be able to improve the performance and results of pedagogical coordination management, and at the same time improve the working environment and the relationship between the coordinator-teacher, coordinator-director and coordinator-parents/guardians, and promote the development of collective human endeavours.

CHAPTER 3

FUNDAMENTALS OF THE COORDINATING TEACHER: INITIAL UNDERSTANDINGS

According to Domingues (2009), schools have taken on the obligation to carry out continuous learning for their teachers, and the Teacher Coordinator is the professional who appears in this scenario as responsible for teacher development. His thesis confirms that the teacher coordinator is the manager of the time and space for ongoing teacher training in São Paulo state schools. The research examines how this manager controls, organises and programmes ongoing training in the collective timetables. The qualitative empirical research involved four pedagogical coordinators, two schools and two groups of teachers during the Special Comprehensive Training Day (JEIF). The dialogue group, organised using a bricolage methodology, sought to listen to the teachers taking part in this training process and their perceptions of this space for action and reflection and the role of the teacher coordinator. The results confirmed the thesis that the work of the CP, according to the focus of the research, *is* a multidetermined 'know-how', resulting from factors such as personal development, institutional organisation and public policies. In addition, they showed the fragility of the coordinator's initial training and the ongoing training offered. They also show that the PC needs time to build a formative identity in order to be able to establish the facet of leadership based on an indeterminate amount of time for their reflective and critical training.

The article by Fernandes (2012) analysed the work of pedagogical coordination in São Paulo state schools in the context of educational reforms between 1996 and 2010, analysed the main resolutions published by the Department of Education on the role of Teacher Coordinator and discussed some of the data obtained from qualitative empirical research carried out in three schools in the final years of primary and secondary education in the interior of São Paulo. The analysis allowed us to recognise the implications of the educational reforms for the role, as well as identifying and interpreting the ways in which the subjects readjusted their management and school organisation work. Pedagogical coordination, identified with the possibility of democratising the school, changing the rigid structures of school administration, and seen as an innovative form of teacher participation in management, capable of expanding the possibilities of collective work and pedagogical articulation, was, with the measures imposed, taking on other tasks and having its nature and identity altered. An analysis of the main resolutions on this function indicates that it was appropriated by the educational reforms, which distorted its objectives and forms of action, making it a function closer to centralised power than to school organisations and subjects. The Teacher Coordinator becomes the "visible eyes" of the education system (Barroso, 2006).

It is also based on another article by Fernandes (2009), which aims to present the results of a study that analysed the creation of the role of teacher pedagogical coordinator (PCP) in São Paulo state schools as part of the educational reforms that took place in the mid-90s. We are guided by a bibliographic-documentary study that analysed documents from the Department of Education (including legislation), materials produced by teachers' representative bodies and a bibliography related to the history of education, which sought to elucidate the path taken by pedagogical coordination in different historical contexts, analysing the conception of teaching work in relation to these moments. On the other hand, the coordinator's difficulties in working in state schools were investigated, using research that had been produced previously on certain topics of interest: a) identity and the specific space in which the Coordinating Teacher works (Clementi, 2001; Mate, 2010; Christov, 2001; Dias-da-Silva; Lourencetti, 2002) and b) the constant deviation of the CP's function (Dias-da-Silva, 2002; Christov, 2001; Clementi, 2001), the analysis of which made it possible to get closer to the working context of the function and to recognise the implications of educational reforms for the constitution of teaching professionalism.

The research presented in the article by Waldmann and Schneltzler (2007) focuses on the binomial Pedagogical Teacher Coordinator (PCC) / Continuing Teacher Education (FDC) in order to investigate the roles, places and conflicts experienced by Teacher Coordinators. The empirical field of this investigation was the interactions that took place in a group made up of five PCs. This is a case study with a qualitative research approach. The audio-recorded interactions were transcribed and analysed in the light of the cultural-historical approach, Bakhtinian enunciation theory and contributions from educational literature on CPs and teacher training. There were ten meetings, each lasting 3.5 hours. From the transcripts of the meetings, episodes were cut out that emphasise the CPs' relationships with other teachers, headmasters, students, staff professionals and other possible bodies (guardianship council, school board and education department) - and episodes relating to HTPC meetings (Collective Pedagogical Work Time). The results show the roles and places of CPs as taskmasters, messengers of authority, intermediaries between headteacher and teacher, bureaucrats, leading to the emergence of obstacles and mismatches in the relationships established with other agents in the school context. However, they also provide assistance to teachers and management, despite developing a FDC characterised by the technical rationality model.

Authors Waldmann and Schneltzler (2007) and Fernandes (2004) share the same view on job deviations due to the various difficulties imposed by work:

> (...) the deviation of function, the absence of identity, the lack of a specific area of activity in the school environment, the isolation from daily work, the deficiency in pedagogical training, the coexistence with a bureaucratised work routine, the use of the function to convey, impose and defend the projects of the Department of Education, the presence of authoritarian and judgmental traits and the weakness of procedures for carrying out collective work. (FERNANDES, 2004)

In the collection on the theme of the Coordinating Teacher and Teacher Training, organised by Bruno, Almeida and Christov (2009), the work of the CP is related to sub-themes such as: continuing training for the coordinating teacher; the locus of this continuing training; teaching reforms; the role of the CP in the relationship with novice teachers; the importance of the CP's leadership and the impact of new technologies on society and the school universe, dealing with how CPs can help teachers to work in a qualified way with these new technologies.

Another collection, "O coordenador pedagógico e o espaço da mudança" (The pedagogical coordinator and the space for change) features articles written by various educators that focus on different aspects involving the PC, and in this one, Christov (2010) contributes a text: "Intentions and problems in pedagogical coordination practices", demonstrating the results obtained from a Freirean proposal for continuing teacher education in three municipalities in the state of São Paulo, taking into account the environment, beliefs and different political and professional trajectories of the PCs investigated. It can be seen that the political space ends up influencing the pedagogical projects and consequently the results credited to the CPs.

Ongoing training in the collective space is also emphasised in Bruno's (2009) text "O trabalho coletivo como espaço de formação" (Collective work as a training space). Reflection and problematisation on the identity of the Teacher Coordinator is present in Mate's (2010) text "What is the identity of the pedagogical teacher coordinator?", which is based on two aspects: the risks of defining the role of PC and the historical significance of the hierarchy of roles in the school institution. Placco (2010) reflects on the Teacher Coordinator in the face of the challenge of being given the task of articulating and mobilising the school team to weave together the collective work of the school, guiding it as a preventive work, and demonstrating that the PC must develop competences that go beyond the bureaucratic function explored by Fernandes (2011).

According to Silva (2012), there is a need to raise awareness of the continuing education of both the Teacher Coordinator and the management team in order to guarantee the quality of teaching. The problem under discussion is to see what the role of pedagogical coordination is in the ongoing training of teachers and how this results in greater political and social commitment to education. The hypotheses observed show their results based on qualitative research through interviews with teachers and professors. Among the hypotheses observed, we highlight the fact that the coordinating teacher's work can encourage the construction of an articulated work that aims to promote the autonomy of the school team, enriching professional practice and fostering the exchange of knowledge; the exchange of experiences and the exercise of dialogue encourage the overcoming of obstacles and problems become stimuli for overcoming new problems and finding new solutions. Continuing Education should be a good alternative to help teachers achieve autonomy in the face of conflict issues that interfere with the teaching-learning process. The aim of this study was to investigate the social political commitment of Teacher Coordinators, analysing their training history, their attributions and their beliefs about continuing education. The results show that there is a conflict between the proposal for continuing training from theory to practice. The social subjects surveyed feel that there are difficulties in exercising autonomy, for various reasons, but mainly because the plans are ready-made and therefore have to be passed on and followed.

Celestino (2012, p. 32) also points out that "the changes demanded by educational reforms, motivated by social changes, also have an impact on the training of education professionals." (CELESTINO, 2012, p.32). (CELESTINO, 2012, p.32) He complements his proposal by saying that "Continuous learning is a requirement these days, and it is necessary to develop the competence to 'learn *to* learn and continue learning' throughout one's professional life." There is a need to coordinate technical-theoretical and practical knowledge in order to form critical citizens, and in the author's opinion, the school is the privileged place for this to happen. In this context, the Teacher Coordinator plays an important role in teacher training and intrinsic leadership. The PC must carry out "[...] coordinated actions in order to resolve weaknesses and enhance the skills and competences that are essential for educators" (CELESTINO, 2012, p.32). According to Celestino (2012, p. 43) Pedagogical Coordination has the difficult but essential task of coordinating, monitoring, advising, supporting and evaluating pedagogical activities, always guided by the priority function of providing pedagogical and didactic assistance to teachers in their respective subjects. Another important function of coordination is to establish a relationship with parents and the community, always seeking the highest ideal, which is the learning of the student, in order to meet their needs and seek personal fulfilment, with responsibility, respect, dignity and the ability to be part of a society without frustration and prejudice. As a leader, the Pedagogical Coordinator must "influence an innovation process in multiple ways and at various stages of a project's life cycle" (CELESTINO, 2012, p. 43), a project which, as already mentioned, is built with the educational community. Its role begins with the construction of the project and extends throughout the implementation process. It "influences the orientation of the project, the formulation of objectives, the right balance between utopia and realism [...] it exerts its influence during the implementation of the collective project, especially when it stumbles over an obstacle, a dilemma or a tactical or strategic problem" (CELESTINO, 2012, p. 43). It can be seen that such action has a significant influence on the constitution and performance of the group of teachers, since the tone that the coordination gives to the work can stimulate or curtail the participation of the teachers and the constituted leaders. The pedagogical coordinator must bear in mind the need to play a conciliatory and integrating role, since their actions can "mobilise and channel everyone's commitment to change, or they can become obstacles or even outright opponents of the project" (CELESTINO, 2012, p. 43).

In his master's dissertation, Lomonico (1980) presents the central object of his research, which was the self-evaluation of the performance of the duties of the Teacher Coordinator in poor schools in the Metropolitan Region of Greater São Paulo. Theoretically, her project was based on the Stuffleabeam-Guba evaluation model (1971; 1973). However, in order to solve the practical problems of "how" to identify and/or "build" instruments suitable for collecting data on the duties performed by the Teacher Coordinator, it was necessary to develop a paradigm for these duties. Criticism and judgements are not made in this work because, according to the point of view of these theorists, such tasks are not the responsibility of the researcher. The following were drawn up: a paradigm of the CP's duties, the categories and indicators of which were surveyed using formal documents in force, and a survey of problems (situations and/or conditions) that could be interfering with the Teacher Coordinator's performance of their duties in their work environment. The population covered 225 (two hundred and twenty-five) PCs in post between 10 August and 10 September 1979. As for the methodological tools, two instruments based on the paradigm and the survey of problems mentioned above were developed and validated in terms of content. The analysis of the results obtained with instrument no. 1 made it possible to characterise the population and verify the hypotheses that guided the work. It also made it possible to point out the particular behaviour of the indicators in the various areas of the paradigm. Analysing the results obtained with instrument 2, we looked at how the CPs perceive the problems (situations and/or conditions) presented. To summarise, the objectives achieved by this work were: to draw up a paradigm of the duties of the Teacher Coordinator defined in the legal provisions in force; to characterise the study population in terms of data: gender, age group, training and years of service in the position; Drawing up instruments for self-assessment of the duties of the CP in deprived schools in the Metropolitan Region of Greater São Paulo; Verifying the hypotheses that guided the work; Surveying the problems (situations and/or conditions) that have interfered in the execution of the CP's duties, and; Providing subsidies to central bodies for the purpose of making decisions regarding planning.

In her article, O professor coordenador pedagógico nas escolas estaduais paulistanas: da articulação pedagógica ao gerenciamento das reformas educacionais, published in the journal Educação e Pesquisa, Fernandes (2012) returns to her main theme, derived from research carried out in 2006 and 2008, with the Teacher Coordinator as the central focus. Based on a bibliographic-documentary study, she analyses the main resolutions published by the São Paulo State Department of Education between 1996 and 2010. To define the period of analysis, the successive educational measures of a neoliberal nature that took place in the school system were taken into account. Based on the selected resolutions, we established some categories of analysis related to the function: name, justification and legal attributions; necessary requirements for coordinating teachers and selection criteria; evaluation of the work carried out and basic bibliography requested in the selection processes. Analysis of the legal documents allows us to identify the appropriation of the role by recent educational reforms, recognising the implications for teaching work and school organisation. Influenced by managerialist and performative principles, the educational reforms have led to profound changes in the nature of the work of the pedagogical coordinator teacher, who, from being an organiser within the school, is now legally responsible for disseminating official measures and controlling teaching activities.

Russo and Carvalho (2012) present the partial results of a study on the educational reforms underway in the state of São Paulo, based on the government's Action Programme for Education and the São Paulo Makes School programme. The research aims to understand the political-pedagogical foundations of the reform as well as its impact on school practice. This text analyses the political-pedagogical foundations, and situates these policies within the regulatory framework founded in the 1990s, starting with the FHC government. It presents the objectives of these policies, highlighting the extent to which they contradict legal precepts that guarantee the didactic-pedagogical autonomy of teachers, presents their creators and, finally, questions their ability to contribute to the effective improvement of São Paulo's public schools. The research presents the ten targets set by the state government for the reform of state public education, to be met by 2010:

1. All 8-year-olds are fully literate.

2. A 50 per cent reduction in the failure rate in grade 8[a] .

3. A 50 per cent reduction in high school failure rates.

4. Implementation of learning recovery programmes in the final grades of all learning cycles (2nd, 4th and 8th grades of primary school and 3rd grade of secondary school).

5. A 10 per cent increase in the performance of primary and secondary schools in national and state assessments.

6. Meeting 100% of the demand from young people and adults for secondary education with a diversified vocational curriculum.

7. Implementation of nine-year primary education, with priority given to the municipalisation of the initial grades (1st to 4th).

8. Continuing education and training programmes for staff.

9. Decentralisation and/or municipalisation of the school feeding programme in the 30 municipalities that are still centralised.

10. Programme of works and improvements to school infrastructure.

According to the Department of Education, this programme would be implemented through ten actions:

1. Implementation of the Read and Write Project;
2. Reorganisation of continuous progression;
3. Curriculum and learning expectations;
4. Learning recovery;
5. High school curriculum diversification;
6. Youth and Adult Education;
7. 9-year primary education;
8. Evaluation systems;
9. Results management and incentive policy; e,

10. Works and investment plan.

Five measures were planned to guarantee the implementation of the established actions:

1. Creation of the coordinating teacher position and selection of 12,000 teachers by December 2007.

2. A competition for 300 new teaching supervisor posts and a review of their duties.

3. Strengthening the role of the school headmaster in leading the process of implementing the management model

4. Creation of a working group to implement 9-year primary education

5. Creation of an organising committee for the State Education Plan.

Item one shows the creation of the role of Teacher Coordinator, and at the same time the production of the Manager's Notebook: School Management and Curriculum, which presents the guidelines for implementing the new educational policies. The text makes it the responsibility of the PC to publicise and implement the curricular proposals it sets out. The Coordinating Teacher has been elevated to the status of the main protagonist in the implementation of the new curriculum proposal, i.e. it is up to him/her in the school sphere to "announce the Proposal, clarify its foundations and principles, lead the school community's reflection and organise the school's planning based on the Proposal." (MURRIE, 2008, p. 6).

Given the primary tasks to be carried out, there was consensus among the authors studied that the Coordinating Teacher is responsible for teacher development, which in the school environment is called Continuous Learning. The Coordinating Teacher is responsible for controlling, organising and programming the time and space for teachers' ongoing training. However, there is the weakness of this professional's initial training, which sometimes comes without specific pedagogical training. There is also the issue of the CP's own ongoing training, which sometimes doesn't focus on the training of managerial leaders and doesn't constitute an elucidated identity. In the meantime, there have been changes to the legislation that guides CPs. These changes, which were made as adjustments to the nature of the political reforms in the state of São Paulo, culminated in alterations to the roles of CPs and, consequently, distorted their objectives and ways of acting, bringing the role closer to centralised power (DE) than to organisations (UE) and school subjects (teachers and students). The CPs are presented with the roles of taskmasters, messengers of authority, intermediaries between management and teachers, bureaucrats and working on the emergence of facts in the school context.

CHAPTER 4

THE COORDINATING TEACHER IN HIS FUNCTIONS AND ATTRIBUTIONS BASED ON THE EVOLUTION OF THE LAWS

The professional in focus in this research has undergone three changes in the nomenclature of his occupation in the public education network since the beginning of its implementation. Firstly, in the 1970s, he took on the position of pedagogical coordinator through a public competition. Then, in the mid-1990s, with the demise of the position and the educational reforms guided by the "New Face School" document, he was renamed Pedagogical Coordinator Teacher. In 2007, he was renamed the Coordinating Teacher, but the role was still maintained.

4.1 SHORT HISTORY OF THE EDUCATION GUIDELINES AND BASES LAW

In recent decades, Brazilian education has undergone several changes in terms of legislation. This has led to the creation of laws and plans that have contributed to the advancement of education in the country. These include the Education Guidelines and Bases Law (LDB 9394/96), the National Education Plan and the 1988 Federal Constitution. The LDB is seen as a legal framework with a major impact on educational institutions, as well as bringing with it a number of innovative elements for Brazilian education.

This new Education Guidelines and Bases Law, Law No. 9.394/96, presents a few elements in a tenuous way, when it emphasises in the proposed framework for teaching professionals and their consequent training, the existence of a professional focused on "administration, planning, inspection, supervision and educational guidance for basic education" (BRASIL, 2001), in the form of a specialist, whose initial training required for the action is higher education in Pedagogy or Postgraduate Studies.

The definition in law of an education professional to provide pedagogical support and specific actions to accompany teaching, in the traditional terms of supervision of basic education, was already dealt with in Law No. 5,692 of 1971, and the aspects of the requirement for their training mentioned in the new LDB also existed in the previous law. In this way, the understanding of the existence of specialists, as a teaching function, is maintained, for which, in the current Law, Art. 67, sole paragraph, teaching experience is a fundamental prerequisite, under the terms of the norms of each education system (BRASIL, 2001).

Article 2 of Resolution No. 03 (CNE-CEB) of 8 October 1997, which sets guidelines for the new Career and Remuneration Plans for the Teaching Profession in the States, Federal District and Municipalities, is coherent and explicit with this legal precept, and reinforces what Law No. 9.394/96 by reaffirming that "professionals who carry out teaching activities and those who offer direct pedagogical support to such activities, including those of school direction or administration, planning, inspection, supervision and educational guidance, are part of the teaching career of the Public Education Systems" (BRASIL, 2010).

Alongside the legal references already mentioned, guidelines for the work of these professionals in educational research have also been established, although they are still timid. From the role of supervisor to pedagogical coordinator within schools, a path of experiences and questions has been traced in search of a new identity for the pedagogical support professional. The search for an identity mentioned here focuses mainly on the construction of a clearer profile or identity for the pedagogical coordinator teacher, the pedagogical support professional present in the daily life of the school.

The aim here is not just to discuss the role of the specialist as a technical function linked to teaching and, in general, as a professional responsible for supervision, in the most traditional terms. We believe it is important to discuss the variation in functions or roles over the course of changes in education and history, and to rediscuss and outline a profile for the pedagogical coordinator in schools, as a professional who is first and foremost a teacher and works in schools. The emergence of this professional is undoubtedly a result of the various attempts to give a new face and profile to the traditional or specialist supervisor.

Supervision, under the name of School Inspection, had already existed in the São Paulo state education system systematically and as a mediator between the school and the higher education administration since the 1950s, continuing the tasks of inspecting school groups from the previous decade.

4.2 EVOLUTION FROM SUPERVISION TO PEDAGOGICAL COORDINATION

Supervision was born with industrialisation and its aim was to improve production in factories and industries. Before it reached the school, it spread to various sectors: the military, health, sports, politics and others, always with the aim of achieving quality and quantity results, in other words, seeking better performance from the school in its educational task (LIMA, 2008, p. 69).

From the 18th to the 20th century, the purpose of supervision was to inspect, repress, check and monitor. At first, in 1841, the proposal of supervision linked to the teaching process emerged, but it was still linked to the verification of teaching activities.

At the beginning of the 20th century, supervision focused on standards of behaviour and criteria for measuring school performance, with a focus on teaching efficiency. It was the beginning of the use of scientific knowledge, so supervision was able to show, transmit, explain and replicate. From 1925 onwards, supervision introduced democratic principles into educational organisations. From 1930 onwards, it took on the character of leadership and decision-making in educational processes. In Brazil, supervision left aside its supervisory nature and appeared for the first time in the Francisco Campos Reform, Decree-Law 19.890 of 18 April 1931.

The Organic Law of Secondary Education, Decree-Law 4.244 of 09/04/1942, art. 75, paragraph 1, formalises this trend: "The inspection will be carried out only from an administrative point of view, but still with the character of pedagogical orientation." On 14/11/1953, by Decree-Law 34.638, inspectors received subsidies for training and grounding their work in schools, with an emphasis on pedagogical character.

With the enactment of Law 4.024 of 20/12/1961, it was established that states and municipalities should take on the organisation and execution of educational services. Within this proposal, the LDB decentralises inspection, leaving it up to the states to organise this service at primary and secondary level, today called Basic Education by the current LDB 9394/96 (Early Childhood Education, Primary Education I and II and Secondary Education).

In 1974, with the Magisterium Statute, the official figure of the Supervisor appeared for the first time in the state of São Paulo - Complementary Law no. 114 of 13 November 1974, and in 1975 and 1976 with Decrees 5.586/75 and 7.510/76 the Supervisor's attributions were defined. Two years later, in 1978, Complementary Law 201/78 introduced the figure of the Supervisor under the name of Teaching Supervisor.

The overall system of the São Paulo state education department is defined in Decree No. 7.510/76, and has the following structure.

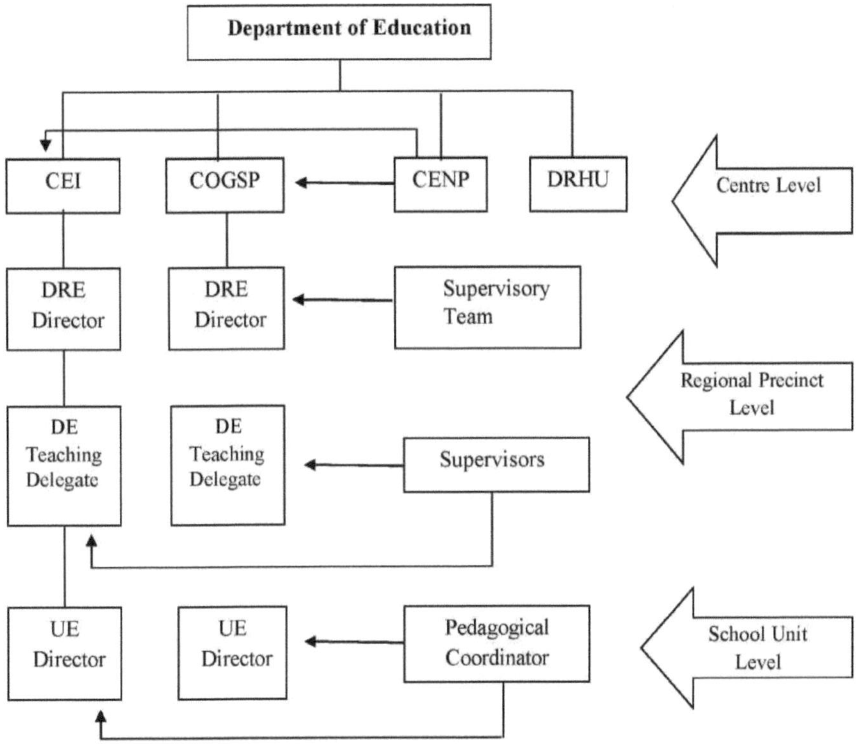

Figure 01: Hierarchical structure of SEESP/1976[3]

At the beginning of 1981, the Department of Education took on the responsibility of holding a public examination to select Teaching Supervisors with a defined field of work, covering early childhood education, special education, 1st and 2nd grade education in the regular, supplementary and vocational modalities for schools and courses in the state, municipal and private networks.

It is important to note that the role of the inspector gradually waned as it was adjusted to changes in laws and reforms. Thus, after the socio-political and educational changes of 1964, which focused on training for the labour market, depoliticisation of members of the teaching community, discouragement of reflection, fragmentation and specialisation of work, the qualification of teaching supervisor took shape. These new professionals are placed to carry out their tasks in technical-administrative bodies, and when they work in a school unit they are called Pedagogical Coordinators.

[3] CEI - Coordenadoria do Ensino do Interior; COGSP - Coordenadoria do Ensino da Região Metropolitana da Grande São Paulo; CENP - Coordenadoria de Estudos e Normas Pedagógicas; DRHU - Departamento de Recursos Humanos; DRE - Divisões Regionais de Ensino; DE - Delegacia de Ensino; UE - Unidade Escolar.

According to Lomonico (2005, p. 9),

> The implementation of the reform of primary and secondary education in the state of São Paulo, in accordance with Law 5.692/71, required an organisation and readjustment of the educational infrastructure, through a series of formal measures (plans, programmes, legal norms), aimed mainly at improving teaching and controlling the dropout rate in the system. In order to achieve these objectives, the first pedagogical coordinators were introduced into the system, the element of supervision at school unit level.

This Coordinator would initially assist the neediest schools that presented SEESP with a project specifying the EU's physical conditions, number of pupils per class, number of periods and even human resources.

The Coordinator's duties, initially defined by Decrees 5.586/75 and 7.709/76, should cover four areas: planning, assistance, in-service training and evaluation. These include the following basic duties:

Planning
- Planning activities for which the school is responsible.
Assistance
- Ensuring the efficiency and effectiveness of teacher performance
Training
- Improving teaching standards.
Evaluation
- Evaluate teaching results.

Figure 02 - Basic duties of the Pedagogical Coordinator Decrees 5.586/75 and 7.709/76

1° Plan the activities for which the school is responsible:
- Participation in drawing up the school plan, as a PC;
- Monitoring and controlling the development of the curriculum programme.

2° Ensure the efficiency and effectiveness of the teacher's performance, whose tasks are:
- Provide technical assistance to the teacher;
- Planning teacher development and updating activities;
- Coordinating the planning, execution and evaluation of teachers' meetings;
- Interpreting the system's rules and regulations regarding technical-pedagogical aspects.

3° To improve teaching standards, the tasks of which are:

- Coordinating recovery activities;
- Supervising working hours;

- Plan small experiments and surveys;
- Coordinating class and/or grade council meetings.

- ° **Evaluating the results of teaching, including the tasks:**
- Controlling the variables of the teaching-learning process;
- Evaluating the product of the teaching-learning process (LOMONICO, 2005, p. 28).

Lomonico (2005, p. 27) also shows that in order for the four areas to be established, as well as the task indicators (attributions), it was necessary to raise formal documents drawn up by the Human Resources Department (1976), the Pedagogical Studies and Standards Coordination Office (1978) and the model for the coordinator's role proposed by the Rio Grande do Sul Department of Education (1976). The results of these task indicators are presented in the tables in appendices 01a, 01b and 01c at the end of this paper.

There is a pedagogical focus in the tasks to be carried out by the coordinator, who was guided in this first moment by the bibliographic themes for the selection of these first coordinators: aims and values of education, the education system, the functions of supervision, planning, curriculum, instructional processes, educational measures, remedial teaching. (LOMONICO, 2005, p. 20). The introduction of this specialist into the school unit does not compete with the leader who is the headmaster, as the former has no legal authority. However, he does have the delegation of two authorities: authority by competence through professional merit, and authority by delegation, when he receives authorisation from the administrative side to carry out a specific action.

On 18 March 1976, the governor of the state of São Paulo, Paulo Egydio Martins, sanctioned Decree 7709/76 which, in Chapter II, section III, sets out the provisions for the attributions, functions and work of the Pedagogical Coordinator of 1st and 2nd grade schools in the state of São Paulo.

With regard to the professional who will occupy the position of Pedagogical Coordinator, Decree 7709/76 states that the minimum requirements are "to have a university degree corresponding to a full degree in Pedagogy; preferably to have a specific qualification in School Supervision; and to have at least five years of effective teaching in the Teaching Career".

The requirements were more demanding and focused on the candidate's specific training.

Article 3 of Decree 5.586 of February 1975 sets out the duties of this candidate for the position of Pedagogical Coordinator:

> I - carry out tasks relating to the monitoring, evaluation and control of the curriculum;
>
> II - ensure the systematic and regular flow of information on the implementation of curricular activities, enabling feedback on planning at school and system level;
>
> III - take part in drawing up the school plan, coordinating aspects relating to curricular proposals;
>
> IV - coordinating the planning, execution and evaluation of the school's pedagogical meetings;
>
> V - present a diagnosis of the school's curricular activities at the end of each school year. (JUSBRASIL)

Curiously, Article 2 of the same Decree presented the duties of a new position, the Teacher Coordinator, who would be the professional supporting the Pedagogical Coordinator. His duties are described below:

> I - coordinating the activities involved in drawing up the school plan with regard to the specific curricular proposals for their area;
>
> II - to collect information and systematise data specific to their area, to support the monitoring, evaluation and control tasks for which the Pedagogical Coordinator is responsible;
>
> III - forwarding the work plans for their area to the Pedagogical Coordinator and requesting the necessary measures for their implementation;
>
> IV - ensuring the implementation of the action policy defined by the school team, informing all teachers in the area of the working rules established by the team and the calendar of activities, as well as planning, coordinating and evaluating the pedagogical meetings in the area;
>
> V - promote coordination with other areas that make up the school's organisation. (JUSBRASIL)

It can be seen that Decree No. 5,586 includes the functions of Pedagogical Coordinator and Teacher Coordinator, explaining their duties in its articles. Thirty years later, in SE Resolution 88 of 19/12/2007, we see that there will no longer be a Pedagogical Coordinator, and thus the title Teacher Coordinator, explained as a gratified position that will take over all the previously divided attributions.

These changes in titles came in a sequence of renewed resolutions and laws. What is understood today is that in São Paulo state public schools, this professional's position is called Teacher Coordinator. Previously, with the publication of the São Paulo Teacher Education Statute in 1985, it was Teacher Pedagogical Coordinator and in the previous Statute, from 1974, Pedagogical Coordinator.

The wave of changes extends to the requirements for hiring this professional. In SE Resolution No. 88 of 19/12/2007, in relation to the prerequisites necessary for this professional to work, in the city of São Paulo, private and public schools in the municipal network require a degree in Pedagogy or a Master's in Education. On the other hand, in the state network there is no such requirement. For a teacher to be appointed as a Coordinating Teacher, they only need to have a full degree, a minimum of three years' teaching experience (in the state network) and have passed a selection test. Another difference is in the form of selection: in the municipal network, the pedagogical coordinator joins by means of a competition to fill a position. In the state network, it is by appointment to a position, continuing with the teaching post and returning to it if their appointment is terminated. This is not the case with the positions of teaching supervisor and headteacher, which are posts.

However, SE Resolution No. 3 of 18/01/2013, when creating the position of Teacher Pedagogical Management Support Coordinator, returned to Decree 7709/76, in the question that indicates the minimum training to exercise the functions of pedagogical coordinator, "to have a higher education degree corresponding to a full degree in Pedagogy", maintaining a change from five to three years of experience in the teaching profession of the State Department of Education.

Only six months later, the issue of the lack of definition of the minimum training for candidates for the position of Teacher Coordinator was revisited. On 3 June 2013, the Official Gazette (D.O.E. - Executive I - 04-06-2013 - p. 32) published a text amending the provisions of SE Resolution No. 3 of 18 January 2013. The text of SE Resolution No. 35/2013 explains that:

> The Secretary of Education resolves:
>
> Article 1 - Item I of Article 7 of SE Resolution No. 3, of 18.1.2013, shall come into force with the following wording:
>
> Article 7

> "I - hold a full degree in Pedagogy or a Higher Normal course, or a certificate of completion of a postgraduate course in Education, duly authorised by the competent body, and take part in the selection/classification process to be organised, carried out and assessed by a commission to be appointed by the Regional Education Director;" Article 2 - This resolution shall enter into force on the date of its publication, and any provisions to the contrary, in particular SE Resolution No. 18 of 4 April 2013, shall be revoked.

A precedent has been set so that professionals with a degree can apply to become a Pedagogical Management Support Coordinator Teacher.

It is necessary to clarify pedagogical coordination in the state of São Paulo, since this state prioritised the legal and technical separation between school supervision, pedagogical coordination and teacher pedagogical coordinator in the early 1970s, unlike other Brazilian states.

It is understood that the supervisor's work is centred on work units (Education Directorates) and the monitoring of a varied number of schools, while pedagogical coordination is a legally established position that has been practically extinct since the end of the 70s. There is also the position of pedagogical coordinator, held by a teacher elected from among his or her peers, who coordinates and monitors pedagogical activities in schools.

It should also be noted that in the hierarchical structure of the São Paulo education network there are positions and functions. Positions are filled by means of a public examination for tests and titles, regulated by public notices that allow the successful candidate to take up a position in the state civil service, guaranteeing job stability and incorporation into the staff of the Department of Education. The position is always a temporary occupation because it is not linked to a public competition for entry and promotion, so it is not legally foreseen as a position to be occupied for an indefinite period of time. Access to a position is through appointments, i.e. authorisations for an employee of the Department of Education to temporarily carry out activities provided for in the Teachers' Statute.

The Coordinating Teacher who occupies this position does not enjoy any professional security or stability, since he or she is chosen to occupy the position and can, at any time, be asked to decline it.

CHAPTER 5

RESEARCH METHODS AND TECHNIQUES

In the first phase of the study, a descriptive, qualitative, documentary study was carried out by reviewing the legislation that covers the Coordinating Teacher, in order to systematise the evolution and trajectory of this professional (SEVERINO, 2002; SILVEIRA et al., 2009). To this end, the Law of Guidelines and Bases of Education (LDB), the statutes and resolutions of São Paulo were considered. This legislation was then compared in order to identify the evolution and similarities that could illustrate the trajectory of the subject in terms of the relationships and significant definitions of the duties of the pedagogical coordinator. The first phase of this documentary research surveyed and analysed the laws that guide the PC and was carried out between May 2012 and April 2013. The Resolutions of the São Paulo State Secretariat (SE No. 88/2007, SE No. 90/2007, SE No. 81/2009, SE No. 22/2012, SE No. 3/2012 and SE No. 3/2013) were researched, considering any relevant mentions that touch on the object of study, filtering the keywords: pedagogical coordinator, coordinating teacher and coordinating teacher to support pedagogical coordination.

In the second phase of the study, using a qualitative, descriptive study, a semi-structured interview was carried out, using a script or agenda, with open and closed questions, to find out the knowledge of the actors in this research about the legislation that guides them in their duties (SILVEIRA et al., 2009), (SILVEIRA et al., 2009) Also at this stage of the study, a semi-structured questionnaire was used, with open and closed questions, in order to gain an understanding of the quality and distribution of the time dedicated to teaching and administrative duties (SEVERINO, 2002; SILVEIRA et al., 2009). At the same stage, using an open question, the Coordinating Teachers made suggestions for improving the management of these duties. These interviews were recorded with the consent of the respondents. The collection instrument can be found in Appendix 1. To access the data during phase two of this research, two collection instruments were drawn up:

A) Questionnaire with semi-structured closed and open questions.

The presentation of the research questionnaire observed its origin and purpose in accordance with the ethical theories of scientific work. The first part of the survey began by collecting data on the interviewee. There were gaps so that the interviewee could fill in the fields for identification and maximum current education. Length of service as a teacher, teacher coordinator and/or teacher coordinator of pedagogical management support. Their current professional category and the segment in which they worked. Gender and age were also analysed.

The second part of the survey began with a semi-structured questionnaire with closed and open questions. Questions one and two were about knowledge of the legislation that guides the duties of the Teacher Coordinator (SE No. 88/2007) and the Teacher Coordinator for Pedagogical Management Support (SE No. 3/2013). The interviewee had to answer whether they knew the resolution. If they answered that they knew it, they had to write down their knowledge briefly.

Question three asked the interviewee to assess the amount of time they had to deal with their teachers' pedagogical queries. They had to state whether this time was sufficient or insufficient, and based on this identification, justify their understanding and clarify their position.

Question number four asked the interviewee to assess the amount of time he had for the didactic and pedagogical training of his teachers. They had to state whether this time was sufficient or insufficient, and based on this identification, justify their understanding and clarify their position.

Question five asked the interviewee to assess the time they had to resolve administrative issues. They had to state whether this time was sufficient or insufficient, and based on this identification, justify their understanding and clarify their position.

Question number six asked the interviewee to give suggestions for improving the performance of their activities in terms of time to clarify pedagogical doubts of their teachers, carry out didactic and pedagogical training of their teachers, and resolve administrative issues.

To this end, the social subjects of the research were selected on the basis of intentional, quality sampling criteria, seeking to study coordinating teachers of primary and secondary public education in the state network of the city of Mauá, located in the state of São Paulo, who presented quality in terms of knowledge about the role and attribution in the performance of the position they held. In view of this, the research form containing the agenda of questions was given to eleven coordinating teachers who had been in the position for at least a year, and they were selected by the Education Directorate responsible for the academic and administrative management of state primary and secondary schools in the region of the city of Mauá, in the state of São Paulo.

In the third phase of the study, using a Work Distribution Chart (ALVAREZ, 1990), the Teacher Coordinators wrote down their main activities during a working week, every hour. The document for this data collection can be found in Appendix 2. Activity Diary - Work Distribution Chart (QDT). At this stage of the research process, each interviewee received, electronically, an Activity Diary based on a simplified form of the instrument known as the Work Distribution Chart (QDT), which originated in the discipline of Systems and Methods Organisation. This tool helps to identify the tasks performed, and "represents the distribution of work and has as its main objectives a balanced use of resources based on an approximate distribution of activities, with the aim of obtaining balanced results." SIMCSIK (2001). In this survey instrument, the interviewee had to fill in the spaces marked with the main activities they carried out, hour by hour, during a working week.

In its preface, the instrument presented the aim of the research and contained a gap for identifying the respondent. Next, the respondent was given suggestions on how to complete the questionnaire. On the following pages, the respondent had to fill in the spaces in the Activity Diary as requested.

In the fourth phase of the research, the collected data was analysed, based on Bardin's (1971) recommendations, in order to analyse the content of the legislation and the notes on the answers contained in the interview scripts with the Teacher Coordinators, which were duly transcribed. Based on this research result, the work was consolidated into a proposal for intervention and practice for educational management, in the sense of presenting a list of proposals aimed at broadening and consolidating the understanding of the role of the coordinating teacher in schools, in terms of their functions and attributions in school management.

Figure 3 below illustrates the methodological approach adopted.

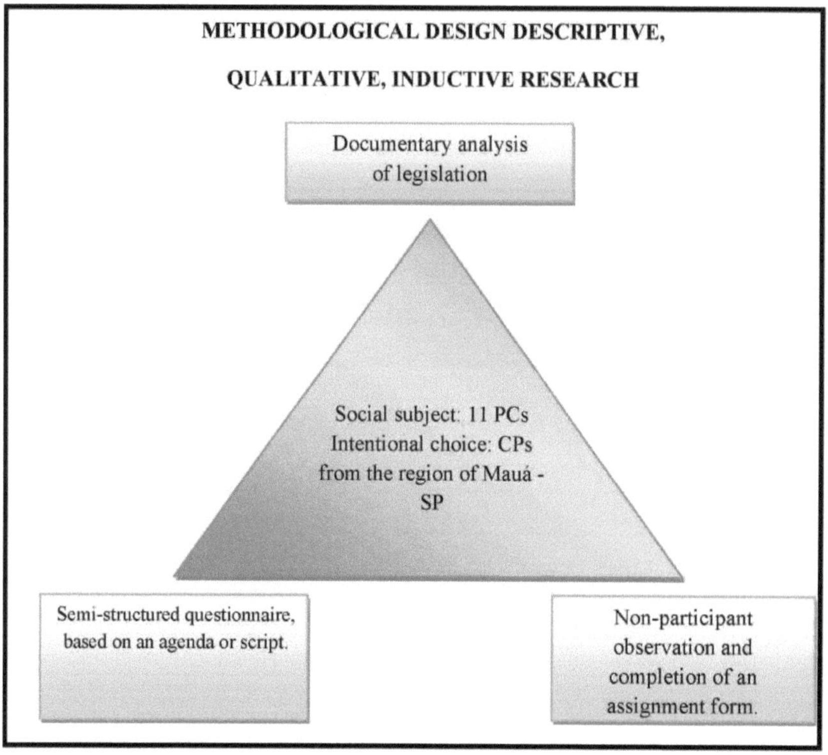

Figure 03: Methodological design of the research

To back up what has been outlined here, it is important to understand that research is one of the ways of creating knowledge and that this has been structured over the years by improving techniques and methodologies for studying its objects and methods. According to Demo (1994, p.20) theoretical research is carried out with the aim of reconstructing theory, concepts, ideas, ideologies, polemics, with the immediate aim of improving theoretical foundations. This research may not be used immediately to intervene in society, but it does provide the conditions for this to happen. Still according to Demo (1994, p.36), "Adequate theoretical knowledge entails conceptual rigour, accurate analysis, logical performance, diversified argumentation and explanatory capacity".

Empirical research focuses on the "empirical and factual face of reality" (Demo, 1994, p.21). This methodology is important because it offers greater solidity to arguments, since the basis and meaning of empirical data is always linked to the theoretical framework, and this data contributes to pertinent changes, since it facilitates the approximation of practice.

The research has a theoretical-empirical design, since implementation evaluation, insofar as it analyses processes, favours a qualitative approach, and it is important to initially highlight some issues that are relevant to understanding the nature of this research, such as the fact that the object of the social and human sciences is historical, i.e. human societies exist in a certain space and time whose social and cultural formation is specific.

From this perspective, according to Minayo (2001, p.39):

> All social research needs to take into account human historicity: (...) respecting the specificity of culture, which carries within itself, and in a complex way, the traces of short, medium and long-term events, expressed in its material and symbolic goods. Society and individuals have a historical consciousness, i.e. what gives meaning to intellectual work is the human being, groups and society itself give meaning to and interpret their actions.

Another characteristic of the social sciences and the humanities is that their "object" of study is made up of a subject, who for cultural reasons, class, age, religion or any other reason, has a common substrate of identity with the researcher. In the words of Minayo (2001, p.42), "The world view of both is implicated in the entire process of knowledge, from the conception of the object to the result of the work".

Social research uses different methods in a complementary way.
In this research we will use the qualitative method, which is applied to the study of relationships, representations, perceptions and opinions, which are products of the interpretations that people make of social life.

As this research is qualitative, this method was adopted to understand and describe phenomena. Originating in the fields of anthropology and sociology in the 1930s, this methodology gradually found its way into the fields of psychology, education and business administration.

Qualitative research provides descriptive data through the researcher's direct and interactive contact with the situation of the object of study. It will be common for the researcher to try to understand the observed event through the perspective of the participants, and then, from this collected material, to situate their interpretation of the facts.

Qualitative research differs in terms of method, form and objectives. Godoy (1995, p.62) emphasises the variation between qualitative studies and lists a set of essential characteristics that will identify a study of this nature.

- The natural environment as the direct source of data collection and the researcher as the fundamental instrument;

- Descriptive character;

- The meaning that people give to things and to their lives as the researcher's concern;

- Inductive approach.

The term qualitative research has different meanings in the field of social sciences. It comprises a set of different interpretative techniques aimed at describing and decoding the components of a complex system of meanings. It aims to translate and express the meaning of phenomena in the social world; it is mobilised to reduce the distance between the indicator and the indicated; between theory and data; between context and action.

The development of qualitative research presupposes a temporal-spatial cut of a given phenomenon by the researcher, and this cut will define the field and the extent to which this research will take place, in other words, the field that will be mapped. In this qualitative study, description is fundamental, because it is through description that the data will be collected (NEVES, 1996).

In turn, using questionnaires, interviews and observations, descriptive research is characterised as studies that seek to determine status, opinions or future projections through the responses obtained. Their value is based on the premise that problems can be solved and practices improved by describing and analysing objective and direct observations. According to Trivinos (1987),

> Descriptive research requires the researcher to have a series of information about what they want to research. This type of study aims to describe the facts and phenomena of a given reality. Examples of descriptive research are: case studies, documentary analysis, ex-post-facto research.

Still for Trivinos, (1987, p. 112),

> [...] descriptive studies can be criticised because there can be an exact description of phenomena and facts. These are beyond the possibility of verification through observation. According to the author, sometimes the researcher doesn't critically examine the information, and the results can be wrong; and the data collection techniques, such as questionnaires, scales and interviews, can be subjective, only quantifiable, generating inaccuracy.

In order to analyse the data collected, in the world of qualitative research, the choice of method and techniques for analysing data must necessarily provide a multifaceted view of all the data collected during the collection period (corpus). This is invariably due to the plurality of meanings attributed to the producer of such data, in other words, its polysemic nature in a naturalistic approach. One method widely used to analyse qualitative data is content analysis, understood as a set of research techniques whose aim is to find the meaning or meanings of a document. The technique is made up of a set of methodological tools that can be applied to various discourses. According to Bardin (1971), the result of these associated techniques is the "extraction of structures translatable into models - it is a controlled hermeneutics, based on deduction: inference". The analysis is validated by the effort to interpret what is retained, in an undeclared form, by the message. And the researcher, for his part, must make his analysis underpinned by both the rigour of objectivity and the fertility of subjectivity.

In this way, Bardin (1971) defines content analysis as a set of techniques for analysing communications, which uses systematic and objective procedures to describe the content of messages. However, the author herself claims that this concept is not enough to define the specificity of the technique, adding that the intention is to infer knowledge about the conditions of production (or, possibly, reception). This inference is based on quantitative or non-quantitative indicators. Content analysis is a set of techniques for analysing communications (BARDIN, 1971).

Following this reasoning, the technique of content analysis refers to the study of both the content in figures of speech, reticence, between the lines, and the explicit messages.

This research followed the phases determined for content analysis:

- Floating reading to pre-explore the corpus of interviews. In floating reading, one makes contact with the documents to be analysed, gets to know the context and lets impressions and orientations flow (BARDIN, 1971).

- Selection of the words, phrases, sentences, expressions that are most frequently quoted in the answers presented in the interview script.

- Selection of Meaning Units (US). The words, phrases, sentences, expressions, among others, that appeared during the readings of the interview scripts were separated into groups.

- The process of categorisation and subcategorisation. Categorisation, according to Bardin (1971), is "an operation of classifying the constituent elements of a set by differentiation and then by regrouping according to genre". In this grouping, two tables will be formed: Units of Meaning and Formation of Categories.

- Content Analysis and Results Analysis. In this phase, the categories surveyed will be compared with the data from the theoretical references presented in the research.

As the aim of qualitative research is to understand the phenomenon being studied from the perspective of the participants in the situation being studied, it takes on different meanings in the field of social sciences. It comprises different ways and techniques for analysing an event. It is essential to understand that "sign and meaning, knowledge and phenomenon, always depend on the framework of interpretation employed by the researcher". (NEVES, 1996, p. 2) On the other hand, qualitative researchers are more concerned with the social process than the social structure, they seek to show the context of the research, and if possible, to have an empathetic approach to the process so that they better understand the procedure of the fact. The attraction that qualitative methods have for researchers and readers is almost undeniable. For this reason, attention must also be paid to possible biases in relation to the observer's view during the research, transcription of the facts and analysis of the phenomenon.

CHAPTER 6

RESEARCH RESULTS

The research carried out between April and June 2013 began with a data collection instrument based on Silveira (2009) and Severino (2002). In this phase of collecting and tabulating the elements of the report, the results obtained from eleven respondents were considered.

This brings the total to eleven Teacher Coordinators who are actively working in this role, ten of whom are female and one male, aged between thirty-four and fifty. Nine of the respondents have a degree in Languages, one in Pedagogy and one in Maths. Four of them have postgraduate degrees, two of which are in the area of Languages, one in Psychopedagogy and one in Maths. There is also one respondent with a Master's degree in Literature. Only one respondent indicated his professional category as Permanent. The length of service as a teacher among the respondents ranges from ten to thirty-four years. The length of service as a Coordinating Teacher ranges from one to nineteen years. No respondent indicated that they had worked as a Teacher Coordinator for Pedagogical Management Support. Seven of the respondents work in the Elementary School Cycle II, and seven of them indicated that they work in the Secondary School Cycle. Below are the graphs illustrating the results and their percentages.

Summary of the Respondents' profile:

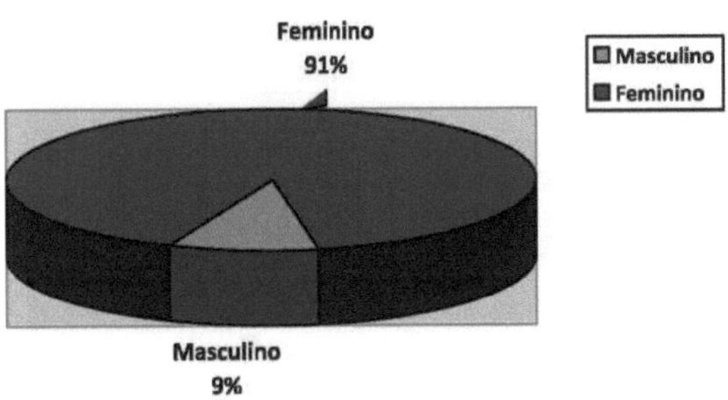

Graph 01 - Distribution by Gender

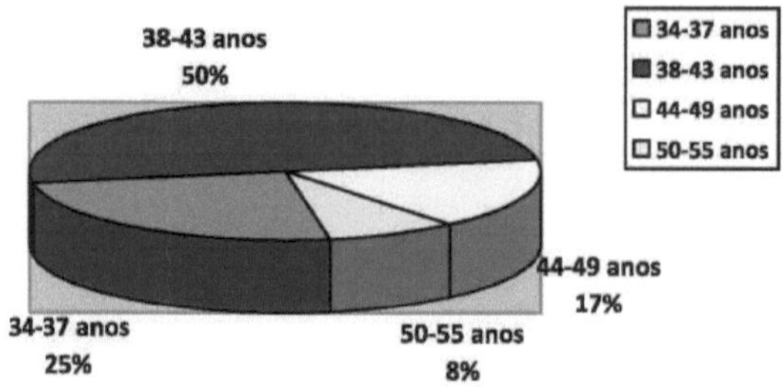

Graph 02 - Distribution by age

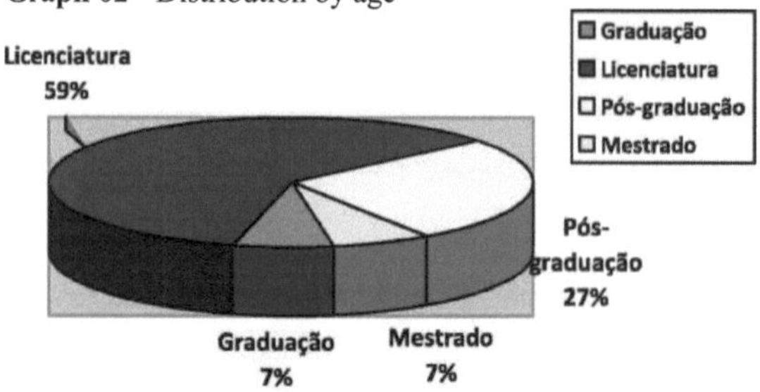

Graph 03 - Distribution by schooling

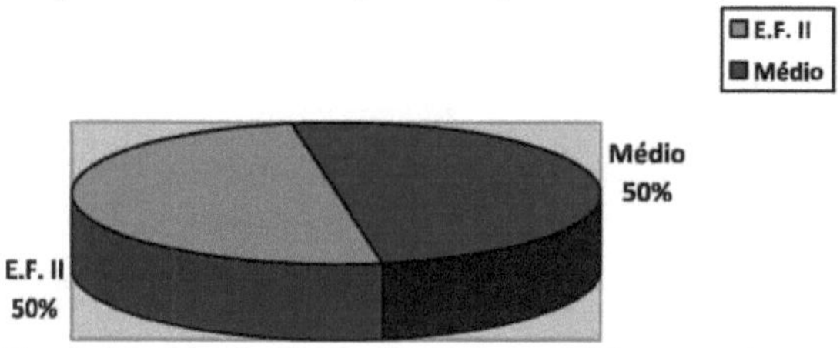

Graph 04 - Distribution by the cycle in which you work as a Coordinating Teacher

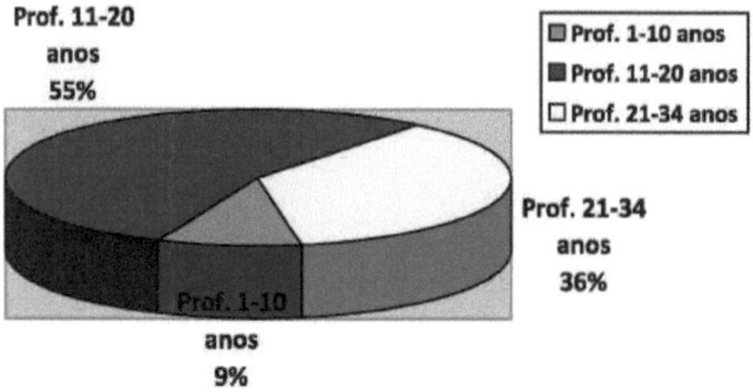

Graph 05 - Distribution by length of service as a teacher

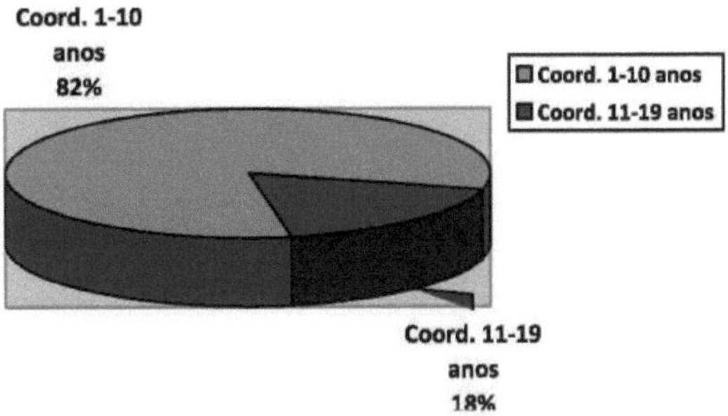

Graph 06 - Distribution by length of service as Coordinating Teacher

6.1 KNOWLEDGE OF LEGISLATION

The first two questions in the survey refer to the interviewee's knowledge of the legislation that guides them. Two questions with the same content were asked about two Resolutions from the São Paulo State Secretariat: SE 88/2007, published on 21/12/2007 and SE 3/2013, published on 18/01/2013. The first Resolution provides for the bonus position of Teacher Coordinator, and the second provides for mechanisms to support the school's pedagogical management in order to implement the actions established by the Education - São Paulo Commitment Programme, including the creation of a new role: Teacher Coordinator for Pedagogical Management Support.

On the first question:

1. Are you aware of SE Resolution 88/2007? ( ) YES ( ) NO If you ticked YES, please briefly write down which parts of this Resolution you know.

Respondents 01, 02, 03, 05, 07 and 10 said they were aware of the Resolution. Respondents 04, 06, 08, 09 and 11 said they had no knowledge. It can be seen that PC 04 and 09 are the respondents with more than five years' experience working as a Coordinating Teacher, and both have postgraduate qualifications.

Of the respondents who said they were familiar with SE Resolution 88/2007, they summarised it by saying that it deals with the role of the coordinating teacher and the pedagogical coordinator. Respondent 01 reported some of the duties contained in the Resolution, but did not mention who they were aimed at. In general, the respondents who said they knew the Resolution gave their answers without giving specific details. There was almost a tie between those who knew and those who didn't know about SE Resolution 88/2007.

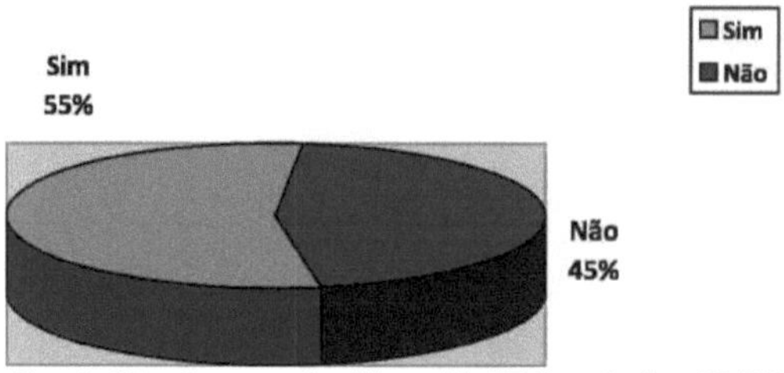

Graph 07 - Are you familiar with SE Resolution 88/2007?

In the second question:

2. Are you aware of SE Resolution 3/2013? ( ) YES ( ) NO If you ticked YES, please briefly write down which parts of this Resolution you know.

Respondents 01, 02, 03, 05, 09 and 10 say they know about SE Resolution 3/2013, while respondents 04, 06, 07, 08 and 11 say they don't know about it. Respondent 03 says that this Resolution is about the new role of the Teacher Coordinator, the Management Support Teacher Coordinator, while respondent 02 says that the Resolution is about the role of the management support coordinator. Respondent 09 adds that this resolution presents the qualifications of the School Management Support Coordinator Teacher. Respondent 01 reports that the Resolution is about implementing mechanisms to support the implementation of a work methodology that is suited to the conditions in each school.

There was almost a tie between those who knew and those who didn't know about SE Resolution 3/2013.

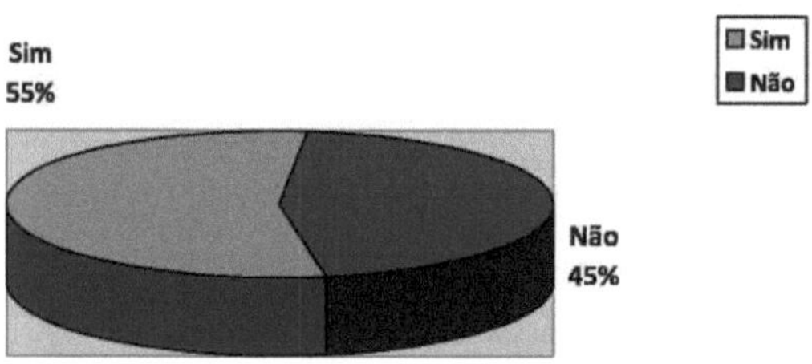

Graph 08 - Are you familiar with SE Resolution 3/2013?

6.2 EVALUATION OF WORKING TIME DISTRIBUTION

In the next three questions, numbers three, four and five, the Coordinating Teachers are asked about the time they have available to dedicate to the duties set out in SE Resolution 88/2007, when Article 2 states that "**The** teacher appointed to the position of Coordinating Teacher will have the following **duties**:"

I - **monitoring** and **evaluating** the teaching and learning process, as well as the results of student performance;

II - **act to** make the actions of pedagogical coordination a collective space for the permanent construction of teaching practice;

III - **take on** the work of continuing education, starting with the diagnosis of teachers' knowledge, to **guarantee** situations of study and reflection on pedagogical practice, encouraging teachers to invest in their professional development;

IV - **to ensure** the active participation of all teachers in the segment/level being coordinated, **guaranteeing** productive and inclusive work;

V - **organising** and **selecting** materials suitable for different teaching and learning situations;

VI - to learn about recent theoretical references relating to teaching and learning processes in order to **guide** teachers;

VII - **disseminate** innovative practices, encouraging the use of available technological resources. (SE No. 88/2007)

In all of the items in the aforementioned resolution, the focus is on continuing education in order to develop teachers' skills and awareness.

With this in mind, the third question arises:

3. In your role as Teacher Coordinator, how do you rate the time available for dealing with your teachers' pedagogical queries? ( ) SUFFICIENT ( ) INSUFFICIENT Please justify your understanding by clarifying your position briefly.

Respondents 01, 02, 05, 06, 07, 08, 09, 10 and 11 say that the time is insufficient, while respondents 03 and 04 say that it is sufficient. Teacher Coordinators 02 and 03 explain that the ATPC is the place (moment) for this, however, the time dedicated to this activity is short because other things come up during the ATPC. PC 03 justifies that he solves the time issue by directing the teacher to reflect on the problem based on theoretical foundations. PC 04 says that he leaves time in his routine for this and that his school unit is small. Respondents 01, 05 and 06 believe that there is a need to raise discussions to answer questions during ATPCs, but that sometimes there are too many subjects to cover and time is short. Respondents 01 and 02 believe that attendance would be more fruitful if it could be done individually. Respondent 07 addresses the issue of teachers' lack of autonomy, which overburdens the pedagogical coordinator with simple issues. Respondent 08 believes that the problem of time lies in accumulating two functions: teaching and pedagogical coordination with the teachers. PC 09 justifies himself by saying that sometimes he has to carry out work requested by the administration, which takes him away from his pedagogical work with the teachers. Respondent 10 says that even with his planning to attend to teachers, time is short. Respondent 11 believes that the problem lies in his lack of experience and the wide range of activities he carries out during his working day as a PC.

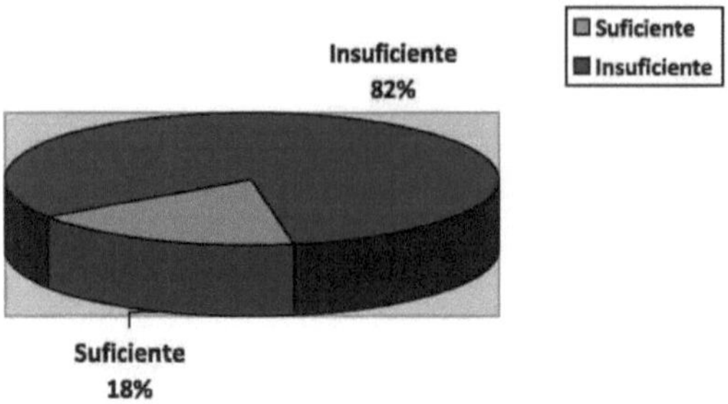

Graph 09 - Distribution of time available to answer teachers' pedagogical questions

In the fourth question:

4. In your role as Teacher Coordinator, how do you rate the time available for didactic and pedagogical training for your teachers? ( ) SUFFICIENT ( ) INSUFFICIENT Please justify your understanding by clarifying your position briefly.

All the Teacher Coordinators say that the time is insufficient. CP 01 clarifies by saying that due to the demand for services, training takes a back seat. PC 02 repeats that time is lacking, and that there should be more ATPC time for pedagogical and didactic training. PC 03 believes that training requires capacity building and not just theoretical studies that take place in the ATPC, and adds that there is no frequency for this to happen. PCs 04 and 06 justify themselves by saying that the work (training) is restricted to ATPC time, and PCs 04 and 08 add that some (teachers) only do (training) for two hours, and this time is very short. PC 11, in addition to agreeing with the previous statement, exemplifies that the meetings are divided between giving messages, training and organising the agenda for the following week.

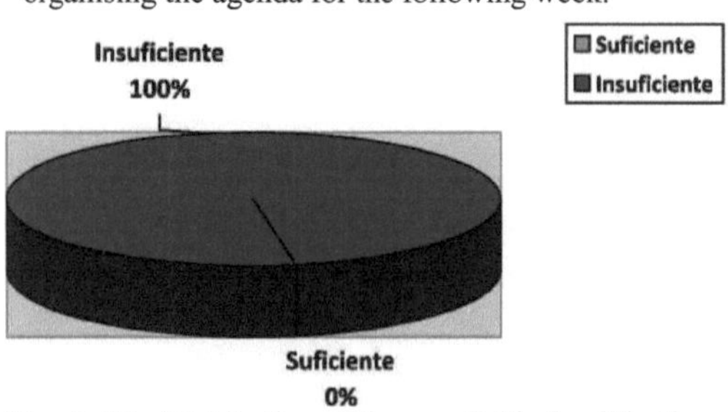

Graph 10 - Distribution of time available for didactic and pedagogical training

In the fifth question:

4. In your role as Teacher Coordinator, how do you rate the time available for didactic and pedagogical training for your teachers? ( ) SUFFICIENT ( ) INSUFFICIENT Please justify your understanding by clarifying your position briefly.

Teacher Coordinators 01, 03, 04, 05, 08, 10 and 11 said that the time is sufficient, while PCs

06, 07 and 09 said that the time is insufficient. PC 02 didn't tick any options, but justified himself by saying that "the Coordinating Teacher doesn't have to deal with administrative issues, but in practice we end up having a deviation of function, resolving the most diverse issues within the school". PCs 01 and 05 agree with PC 02's statement, saying that the coordinator currently has to deal with a lot of administrative issues. The PC says that "[...] I feel that I'm more occupied with administrative matters, lacking time to develop pedagogical work". However, PC 03 countered by saying that "[...] as far as the role of coordinating teacher is concerned, there are few administrative issues". PCs 04 and 08 say that administrative matters are mostly carried out by the headmaster and vice-principal. PC 10 says that he doesn't deal with administrative issues, although he "does tasks that shouldn't be mine, such as checking teachers' points and medical certificates". PC 11 believes that "I've managed the administrative side of things in the first half of the year", but thinks that "I'd need more time for pedagogical issues". He explains that he is adapting due to his lack of experience in the position. PCs 06, 07 and 09 say that there is not enough time for administrative matters because the solution to problems sometimes depends on a third party. PC 06 says that he has already exceeded his working hours in order to meet deadlines and administrative obligations. PC 11 says that he "resolves administrative issues according to their urgency" and that "Many activities that should be done regularly end up being put aside to fulfil new projects or requests from the teaching directorate".

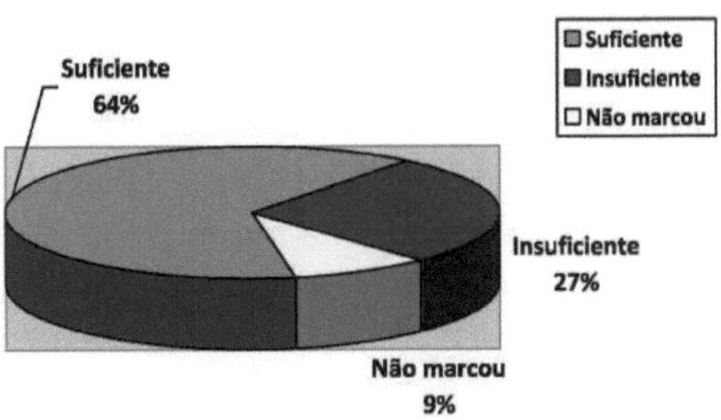

Graph 11 - Distribution of time available to resolve administrative issues

6.3 SUGGESTIONS FOR IMPROVING THE PERFORMANCE OF ACTIVITIES

The final question on the interview agenda asks participants to make suggestions on how to improve their activities, taking into account the scenario they find themselves in.

In the sixth question:

6. Considering the activity of Coordinating Teacher, what suggestions do you have for improving the performance of your activities in terms of time to clarify your teachers' pedagogical doubts, carry out didactic and pedagogical training for your teachers, and resolve administrative issues? Please describe briefly.

PC 01 suggests organising activities according to the workload, while PC 002 lists three topics: "extending ATPC time; promoting continuous training courses for the coordinator, and; 'training' headmasters to help strengthen the figure of the coordinator as a leader in the pedagogical aspect and not with deviations in function". PC 03 suggests more ongoing training for teachers, as this will reduce pedagogical doubts, and administrative issues are dealt with at meetings with managers. PC 004 says that the biggest difficulty is that the ATPCs are held in different groups, which leaves the work fragmented. PC 05 suggests promoting training and continuing education courses for the coordinator, advising people in the school on the real role of the coordinator and creating and organising activities focusing on the coordinator's work time. PC 06 suggests reducing the coordinator's hours as a teacher so that he can carry out his coordination duties. PC 08 agrees with the above proposal and adds that "Taking on two or more roles is extremely stressful and forces us to put aside certain essential things". PC 07 feels that there is a need for better integration with the institution's secretariat in order to facilitate administrative issues, and better organisation of the planning time at the start of the school term. PC 09 believes that for quality work to be carried out, there needs to be time, planning and priorities. He feels the need to "go out into the field" more often and spend more time monitoring the day-to-day work of the teaching staff, attending their classes, giving adequate feedback and carrying out the necessary training. PC 10 says that the issue is really a lack of time. Most of the teachers who are hired are quite inexperienced and need to be monitored more frequently. PC 11 says that he has been taking part in an ongoing training course for a year and that one of the modules was on the use of time. He believes that with practice he will be able to organise himself better and thus make more time available to deal with pedagogical issues with teachers.

6.4 ANALYSING THE DATA COLLECTED

In order for the methodology recommended by Bardin (1971) to be applied efficiently, it is necessary to establish the objectives of the work and delimit the tools that will be used to collect the research. The tools, as described above, will be a documentary study of the Resolutions governing the Coordinating Teacher, interviews in the form of a semi-structured questionnaire and the task distribution chart.

In order to do this, we analysed the points of convergence and divergence between the current legislation on the functions and duties of the CP; identified the functions and duties of the CP in the performance and execution of tasks, in the act of action; compared the current legislation with the performance of the CP, in terms of functions and duties, in their school praxis; and finally, analysed which functions and duties the CP believes they are due to perform at school.

Once these steps had been completed, we began to analyse the content retrieved from the documentary study and the interviews. According to Bardin (1971), in order for the analysis to be carried out carefully, it was necessary to consider certain rules:

> Completeness or non-selectivity, which aims to reduce distortions in interpretations; representativeness, which makes it possible to generalise conclusions; rules of homogeneity, which determine that documents are selected according to strict and well-defined criteria; pertinence, which discusses the suitability of the objects selected for analysis. (BARDIN, 1971)

The material exploration phase followed, which basically consists of coding the material (BARDIN, 1971). Record units were found, which could be words, phrases, symbols, items or documents that led to groups of numbers or quantifications. In the end, the categories for analysis were defined. Still within the categorisation phase, it was possible to take semantic, syntactic, lexical or expressive criteria as a reference (RICHARDSON, 1999).

Working within a quantitative focus, we can observe the presence or absence of certain elements, the constancy with which they appear, the intensity of expression and the direction of the statement.

Then, using the qualitative approach, the presence or absence of certain elements was identified, initiating the phase of the process called processing the results.

The process was closed by the inference and interpretation of the results, when the analysis was closed based on the results obtained in the previous phases and the researcher's inferences (RICHARDSON, 1999).

It was noted that this is a qualitative research proposal, so the recommendations of Richardson (1999) were followed. According to the author, in qualitative research the concern is not to number or measure variables, but to identify them. With regard to the hypothesis, we took as our basis the guidelines of Mattar (1998), who considers that, in qualitative research, the ideal is not to start from a hypothesis, but to generate one at the end of the study.

6.4.1 First Stage of Content Analysis - Identification of Key Words

In the pre-analysis phase, the questionnaires were carefully read and the most commonly used keywords and expressions were identified.

Table 01 - Identification of keywords

Word/Expression	PC 01	PC 02	PC 03	PC 04	PC 05	PC 06	PC 07	PC 08	PC 09	PC 10	PC 11	Total
ATPC meeting	2	1	2	1	0	1	0	0	0	0	1	**8**
Teacher support	1	0	0	0	1	1	0	1	1	1	1	**7**
Training in continuing education	1	0	2	2	1	0	0	0	0	0	1	**7**
Little time / moments / space	1	2	2	3	1	2	1	1	2	2	2	**19**
Fragmented work	1	0	0	1	0	1	1	1	1	0	0	**6**
Tra ining teachers	1	1	1	1	1	1	0	0	0	0	0	**6**
Administrative issues	1	1	1	2	1	1	1	0	1	1	2	**12**
Organising activities	1	1	0	0	0	0	1	1	1	0	0	**5**
Job deviation	0	1	2	0	0	1	1	0	1	1	1	**8**

Table 01 above shows the most important messages and points written by the respondents, since they were given open-ended questions so that they could answer them more freely. Bardin (1977) recommends that it is essential to observe the rules of completeness or non-selectivity of the material read.

A matrix of key words was drawn up in contrast to the questionnaire, which was then used to create units of meaning.

6.4.2 Second Stage of Content Analysis - Formation of Categories and Meaning Units

The intermediate elements of analysis, called units of meaning (US), were identified at this stage from the matrix of key points. The main ideas conveyed by the interviewees were then grouped together, firstly by order of question, then by the similarity of the answers given at various points in the interview. Based on the perception of similarity, frequency and the presence or absence of certain elements in the interviewees' approaches, the meaning units were named. According to Table 02, the following units of meaning (US) were identified.

Chart 02 - Naming of Meaning Units

3. In your role as Teacher Coordinator, how do you rate the time available for dealing with your teachers' pedagogical queries?	
Unit of meaning	**Name**
US1	Insufficient time
US2	Lack of individual moments
US3	Discussion of various problems
US4	Determined time for pedagogical assistance
3. In your role as Teacher Coordinator, how do you rate the time available for didactic and pedagogical training for your teachers?	
Unit of meaning	**Name**
US5	Insufficient time
US6	Moments of study, training, capacity building
US7	They are restricted to ATPC only
3. In your work as a Coordinating Teacher, how do you rate the time available to resolve administrative issues?	
Unit of meaning	**Name**
US8	Enough time
US9	There is a high demand for administrative issues
US10	Deviation in the coordinator's role "PC is a doer of things"
3. Considering *the* activity of Coordinating Teacher, what suggestions do you have for improving the performance of your activities in terms of time to clarify your teachers' pedagogical doubts, carry out didactic and pedagogical training for your teachers, and resolve administrative issues?	
Unit of meaning	**Name**
US11	The ATPC should be used as a space for pedagogical questions
US12	Increase study, training and capacity-building opportunities for teachers
US13	Continuous training courses need to be promoted
US14	Organising the workload
US 15	Avoid accumulating teaching duties
US 16	Avoiding the accumulation of functions outside of coordination

6.4.3 Third Stage of Content Analysis - Creation of Categories

At this stage, a matrix of Categories was created, which according to Bardin (1977) are marks or classes that bring together a group of elements (recording units) under a generic heading, based on the common characteristics of these elements. According to Richardson (1999) the definition of categories by grouping units of meaning should use semantic, syntactic, lexical and expressive criteria. Four categories emerged, as shown in Table 03 below.

Chart 03 - Categories created considering the grouping of Meaning Units

Categories (C)	Meaning Units (US)
Cl Pedagogical work	US1,US2, US11
C2 Teaching time	US5, US7, USI3

C3 Administrative work	US3, US8, US9, US10
C4 Bureaucratic time	US4, US12, US14, US15, US16

6.4.4 Fourth Stage - Content Analysis and Results Analysis

At this stage, the results obtained in matrix 03 were compared with the data found in the dissertation's theoretical framework.

In category **C1** - which corresponds to the **work used by the Coordinating Teachers to attend to teachers' pedagogical questions** - the artefacts **"insufficient time", "lack of individual moments"** and **"ATPC should be used as a space for pedagogical questions"** stand out, which are part of the requests made by the authors Fernandes (2007 and 2011), Waldmann and Schneltzler (2007), Domingues (2009), Magalhães (2011), who contribute to the analysis of the main resolutions on the role of the CP, indicating that the attributions and functions were appropriated by the educational reforms. These reforms distorted the CP's objectives and ways of acting, giving it a role closer to centralised administrative power than to school organisations and subjects in the pedagogical sphere. The emphasis has been shifted away from continuing teacher training and towards managing the roles, places and conflicts experienced by the school's partners.

According to the research Continuing Teacher Education in Brazil: An Analysis of Modalities and Practices, commissioned by the Victor Civita Foundation (2011), "Despite the efforts made in various regions of Brazil by education departments to meet the training needs of school teams, there is still much to be achieved". It is known that it is necessary to guarantee the conditions for pedagogical work to take place in public networks, but according to Gisela Wajskop, in the magazine Nova Escola: Gestão Escolar (2011), "many [schools] institute this formative moment, but they forget to create the necessary structure to make it happen".

PC 01 "Because the space to answer questions is in the ATPC's, where there is a great demand to discuss all the problems in the school. There's no time for the pedagogical part.

PC 02 "I would like to have more time in the meetings (ATPC) and also to have individual moments with the teachers to deal exclusively with pedagogy."

PC 03 "Because when pedagogical doubts are answered, the teacher is directed to reflect on the action/doubt based on a theoretical foundation", "Because training requires training in pedagogical methodologies and not just study, as occurs in the ATPC, because this meeting is a summation of the training that should take place in the school. It's not possible for this to happen very often".

PC 04 "Because the work is restricted to the time of the ATPC's, some only do two hours".

PC 11 "In the two hours a week of ATPC, we have to divide the time between errands, training and organising the weekly schedule for the following week. I think that's too little time.

In category **C2** - which corresponds to the **time CPs have for didactic and pedagogical training for teachers** - the artefacts **"insufficient time", "restricted to ATPC only"** and

"continuous training courses need to be promoted" stood out.

Placco (2010), Almeida (2010), Mate (2009) and Bruno (2009) discuss the identity of the pedagogical coordinator teacher responsible for continuing education. Placco (2010) reflects on the PC when faced with the challenge of being given the task of articulating and mobilising the school team to weave together the school's collective work, guiding it as a preventive effort. Bruno (2009) in the text "Collective work as a training space" states that the CP must develop competences that go beyond the bureaucratic function. She states that "One of the difficulties of collective work lies in confronting the expectations and desires of the subjects involved. This difficulty needs special conditions to be overcome". (BRUNO, 2010, p.16). Christov (2010, p.10) corroborates the topic by stating that continuing education "is a programme made up of different actions such as courses, congresses, seminars, pedagogical working hours (HTPC), technical guidance and individual studies".

PC 01 "Due to the demands of the job, training takes a back seat".

PC 02 "We should have more time to study and prepare lessons with the teachers".

PC 03 "It's not possible for this to happen often".

PC 04 "Work is restricted to ATPC time".

PC 06 "Due to the diversity and volume of tasks, the training sessions are summarised in a few hours at the pedagogical meeting."

PC 08 "The time available for training during term time is really very short, everything is really very busy."

PC 09 "I don't manage to do these training sessions very often, only during specific and sporadic periods."

In category **C3** - which corresponds to the **administrative work involved** in the day-to-day running of the job - the artefacts that stood out **were "There were many bureaucratic tasks (documentation), courses, meeting parents and students, reorganising spaces and materials", "checking teachers' points and medical certificates", "I take care of some administrative issues with the headteacher".** It is part of her daily routine to carry out administrative and bureaucratic work such as monitoring school diaries, scheduling and organising timetables, using the library and classrooms. Scheduling medical appointments and physiotherapy, and promoting excursions, as well as replacing teachers. (Victor Civita Foundation, 2011, p. 27). Oliveira (2009) states that "The pedagogical coordinators who declared that they do some kind of administrative work show that the exercise of these tasks falls into the category of 'helping the *management*'. In this case, the coordinator is subordinate to the decisions made by the headteacher." He goes on to say that "the power in the hands of the headmaster is exercised over the pedagogical coordinator, making him carry out tasks that are not part of his remit due to the lack of other professionals, internally reorganising the tasks carried out in the day-to-day running of the school organisation", such as opening the school, monitoring the entry and exit of pupils, filling in secretarial reports, checking teachers' hours, checking medical certificates and writing statements.

PC 02 "In reality, the teacher coordinator doesn't have to deal with administrative issues, but in practice we end up having a diversion of function, resolving the most diverse issues within the school! The coordinator's work must be respected and not be seen as a 'doer of all things', a problem solver."

In category **C4**, which corresponds to the **time that the Teacher Coordinators have to resolve administrative issues** - the artefacts **"Discussion of various problems", "Sufficient time", "There is a great demand for administrative issues"** and **"Deviation in the coordinator's role 'PC is a doer of things'", "I have often had to go beyond working hours to meet deadlines and administrative obligations"** stood out. In their work, Dias-da-Silva (2002); Christov (2001); Clementi, (2001) reinforce the constant deviation of the CP's function, whose analysis allowed them to get closer to the work context, the function and to recognise the implications of the educational reforms for the constitution of this teacher's professionality. Waldmann and Schneltzler (2007) highlight the roles and places of CPs as taskmasters, messengers of authority, intermediaries between headteachers and teachers, bureaucrats, leading to the emergence of obstacles and mismatches in the relationships established with other agents in the school context. Waldmann and Schneltzler (2007) and Fernandes (2004) share the same view on the deviations of the position due to the various difficulties imposed by the work: "the use of the position to convey, impose and defend the projects of the Department of Education, the presence of authoritarian and judgmental traits and the weakness of procedures for carrying out collective work". Previous studies carried out by Dias-da-Silva and Lourencetti (2002), Clementi (2001), Mate (1998), Christov (2001) and Fernandes (2008) indicated, based on the results of empirical research carried out directly or indirectly with PCPs, that "the position had a fragile identity and a poorly defined space for school activity, i.e. it lacked, in everyday life, a markedly pedagogical territory for action. Without pedagogy as an important reference point, the role came to be identified, in many cases, as one that could coordinate anything within the schools, diverting attention from the main focus of the work to the countless daily tasks present in schools marked by task overload". (FERNADES, 2012)

PC 01 "The coordinator is currently very demanding with administrative issues".

PC 01 and PC 05 "Activities should be organised according to the workload".

PC 02, 03 and 05 suggest "Extending ATPC time, promoting courses for the coordinator's ongoing training [...]", and PC 02 adds, "[...] training" headmasters to help strengthen the figure of the coordinator as a leader in the pedagogical aspect and not with deviations in function".

PC 04 says that "The biggest difficulty is that the ATPCs are carried out in different groups due to the number of classes each teacher has, which leaves the work fragmented

PC 05 "To orientate everyone in the school about the real role of the coordinator".

PC 06 "A significant reduction in my workload as a teacher". PC 08 adds, "Doing two or more jobs is extremely stressful".

PC 07 "Better integration with the school office to facilitate administrative issues".

PC 09 "[...] for quality work to be carried out, you need time, planning and priorities".

PC 10 explains briefly "[...] the issue is really a lack of time to accompany teachers".

PC 11 believes that the more he develops by taking courses, the more he will be able to increase the teaching time for his teachers.

6.5 ACTIVITY DIARIES (QDT)

The Task Distribution Chart tool, according to Alvarez (1990), establishes how many tasks are carried out within a work environment and how many hours are used to carry out these tasks. It can also be used to analyse how much time each employee spends on these tasks. The objectives achieved by this tool, for the purposes of this work, are:

- Identify the activities that consume each employee's time;
- Identify the activities that consume the most of each employee's time.

The objectives derived from the above findings could be:

- Define the most important activity;
- Establish the flow of the main activity;
- Check the flow and continuity of the main activity;
- Identify task overlaps;
- Detect overload or idleness (ALVAREZ, 1990).

6.6 DRAWING UP, FILLING IN AND COLLECTING DATA FROM ACTIVITY DIARIES

The Activity Diary was filled in by the research participants, showing the most important activities they carried out during the working day, every hour, during a working week, from Monday to Friday.

To begin the process, all the Activity Diaries were sorted and, individually, a survey was carried out of the activities presented in the five days of recording. The table below illustrates the research subjects and the hours used for the activities they consider to be the most important of the working day. The records transcribed in the tables below follow the order of the activities transcribed by the respondents.

Tables 04 - Activities and hours used by eleven Coordinating Teachers

PC 01 ACTIVITY	HOURS
Accompanying classes	llh
Raising needs observed in the classroom	Ih
Draw up a script to accompany lessons	3h
Monitoring projects	2h
Talking to teachers	3h
Study legislation	6h
Select material for ATPC	4h
Preparing the ATPC agenda	3h
Observing and evaluating student progress	2h
ATPC	2h
Observe the support teacher's work programme	2h
Collect indicators for analysis	Ih
Draw up possible guidelines in the classroom	1h

PC 02 ACTIVITY	HOURS
Routine organisation	Ih
Attending to disciplinary problems	8h
Classroom monitoring	4h
Attending to parents	5h
Filling in spreadsheets	Ih
Helping to organise the "look at students" outing	4h
Meeting with another coordinator	Ih
Selection of teaching materials for teachers	3h
Preparing copies for teachers	2h
Filling in documents	Ih
ATPC meeting preparation	2h
Monitoring teachers' weekly routines	Ih
Collection of medical certificates/compensation for absences	Ih
Contacting the Guardianship Council	Ih
Assisting the vice-principal with administrative matters	Ih
ATPC	3h
Pedagogical Proposal and Project Studies	1h

PC 03 ACTIVITY	HOURS
Meeting with managers	4h
ATPC	2h
Lunch	5h
Study time	4h
Attending to parents	Ih
Parents' activity	Ih
ATPC	2h
Organisation of the ATPC	4h
Classroom visits	4h

Attending summonses	Ih
Official documents	Ih
Feedback on the monitoring of the Fiaps (resolution 11)	2h
Feedback from room visits	4h
Targeted break monitoring	2h
Preparing events	3h

PC 04 **ACTIVITY**	**HOURS**
Organising the week	Ih
Attending to parents	2h
Meeting with the management team	3h
ATPC	6h
Checking teachers' routines	3h
Monitoring classes	lOh
Organising the ATPC agenda	Ih
Study time	3h
Individual attention for teachers	3h
Feedback to the management team	4h
Meeting at the Directorate of Education	4h

PC 05 **ACTIVITY**	**HOURS**
Checking the day's agenda	Ih
Monitoring disciplinary problems	4h
Class monitoring	3h
Monitoring student departures	4h
Making copies of material for teachers	3h
Filling in documents	3h
Attending to parents	4h
Choosing material for teachers	Ih
Prepare ATPC meeting	2h
Teacher support	6h
Checking documents and absence certificates	2h
Prepare events	Ih
Meeting with the Directorate of Education	3h
ATPC	3h

PC 06 **ACTIVITY**	**HOURS**
General service	Ih
Diary check	Ih
Serving teachers	2h
Meeting with management	4h
Prepare ATPC	2h
Student services	4h
Preparing teacher meeting material	Ih
ATPC	3h
Administrative activities - meeting report	4h
Attending to parents	2h
Visit the classroom	3h
Monitoring student departures	1h

PC 07	ACTIVITY	HOURS
ATPC planning		4h
Meeting with management		6h
Attending to disciplinary problems		3h
Monitoring student departures		2h
Organising Teaching Plans		2h
Attending students		5h
Attending to parents		3h
Filling in documents for the secretariat		6h
ATPC		3h
Visit the classroom		5h
Teacher attendance		Ih
ATPC report		2h

PC 08	ACTIVITY	HOURS
Service to teachers		4h
Classroom visits		3h
ATPC preparation		2h
ATPC		2h
ATPC minutes		2h
Attending students		2h
Feedback to teachers		2h
Preparation of support material		2h
Meeting with management		3h

PC 09	ACTIVITY	HOURS
Visit the classrooms		3h
Administrative documents		2h
Preparing a teachers' meeting		2h
ATPC		6h
Teacher support		2h
Teachers' meeting agenda		Ih
Checking documents - meeting minutes		2h
Filling in spreadsheets		2h
Attending to parents		2h
Disciplinary problems		2h
Monitoring student departures		Ih
Diary check		Ih
Preparing material for teachers		3h
Meeting with management		4h

PC 10	ACTIVITY	HOURS
Individual consultations with teachers		lOh
ATPC planning		2h
Preparation of meeting material		4h
Meeting with management		4h
Attending students		2h
Filling in documents		5h

Classroom visit	2h
ATPC	4h
Attending to parents and students	Ih
Meeting with the Directorate of Education	2h

PC 11	ACTIVITY	HOURS
Organising xeroxes and teachers' folders		5h
Reading e-mails		5h
First semester report card check		2h
Event organisation		Ih
Teacher support		3h
Teacher reception		5h
Attending students		5h
ATPC agenda		2h
Analysing teaching materials		Ih
ATPC		2h
Closing teachers' points		Ih
Lunch		5h
Attending to parents		8h
Preparing the agenda		Ih
Re-planning		3h
Meeting with the technical/pedagogical team		2h
Preparation for next week's ATPC		2h

For the purposes of the maximum number of hours worked per week, forty hours were taken into account, respecting Article. 3 of SE No. 88/2007, which states that "The workload to be carried out by teachers in the role of Teacher Coordinator will be 40 (forty) hours per week".

In the distribution of tasks in the tables above, the subtraction of five hours representing the Teacher Coordinator's lunch hours was taken into account, despite the fact that only two coordinators listed this as a declared activity in the week's diary. It was therefore assumed that everyone worked a total of thirty-five hours that week.

The table below was constructed to identify the activities that required the greatest use of working time during the week surveyed.

Table 05 - Activities with the highest use of hours

PC 01	Accompanying classes	llh
PC 02	Attending to disciplinary problems	8h
PC 03	Meeting with managers	4h
	Study time	4h
	Organisation of the ATPC	4h
	Feedback from classroom visits	4h
	Classroom visits	4h
PC 04	Monitoring classes	lOh

PC 05	Teacher support	6h
PC 06	Student services	4h
	Administrative activities - meeting report	4h
PC 07	Meeting with management	6h
	Filling in documents for the secretariat	6h
PC 08	Teacher support	4h
PC 09	ATPC	6h
PC 10	Individual assistance for teachers	lOh
PC 11	Attending to parents	8h

Next, the activities identified with the highest use of hours during the assessed week were separated. These activities were separated into Administrative Duties and Pedagogical Duties.

The total number of hours used in each of the categories was transformed into a percentage to help with the comparison, considering that 35 hours of work per week corresponds to 100 per cent.

Table 06 - Administrative and pedagogical activities - highest use of hours

PC	**Administrative Activity** **Greater use of hours**	%	**Pedagogical Activity** **Greater use of hours**	%
01	-	-	llh	31,42
02	- - -	- - -	8h	22,85
03	4h	11,42	16h	45,71
04	-	-	lOh	28,57
05	-	-	6h	17,14
06	4h	11,42	4h	11,42
07	12h	34,28	- - -	- - -
08	-		411	11,42
09	-		6h	17,14
10	- - -		lOh	28,57
11	8h	22,85	- - -	- - -

As explained above, for the purposes of comparing this data, all the Teacher Coordinators were considered to have worked 35 hours that week, as recorded in the Activity Log, which represents 100 per cent execution of the tasks.

If you look at the table above, you can see that PC 03 made the most use of his allocated hours for pedagogical tasks, 45.71%, and PCs 06 and 08 made the least use of their allocated hours for pedagogical tasks, with 11.42%. It is also possible to observe that PCs 03 and 06 used the same amount of time to carry out administrative activities, 11.42%, when compared to the minimum time for pedagogical activities. PCs 07 and 11 showed that they paid more attention to administrative tasks, 34.28% and 22.85% respectively. The spaces that were not filled in do not contain activities from any of the categories assessed.

It was also possible to observe the activities and the working time dedicated to them compared to SE Resolution 88/2007, in Article 2:

Chart 07 - Activities compared to the attributions in SE Resolution 88/2007

ATTRIBUTIONS SE no. 88/2007	TASKS RECORDED IN ACTIVITY DIARIES	TOTAL GENERAL HOURS
I - **Monitor** and **evaluate** the teaching and learning pro cess. learning, as well as the results of student performance;	- Accompanying lessons/classroom visits - Teacher support	48h 36h
III - **To take on** the work of continuing education, based on the diagnosis of the knowledge of the students. teachers to **ensure** situations of study and reflection on pedagogical practice, encouraging teachers to invest in their professional development;	- ATPC	32h
V - **organise** and **select** materials suitable for different teaching and learning situations;	- Selection of teaching materials for teachers	23h

In a total of one hundred and thirty-nine hours, it was observed that the Coordinating Teachers use 60 percent of their time to **monitor** and **evaluate** the teaching and learning process, as well as the results of student performance; 23 percent to **take on** the work of continuing training, based on the diagnosis of teachers' knowledge to **guarantee** situations of study and reflection on pedagogical practice, encouraging teachers to invest in their professional development; and finally, 17 percent to **organise** and **select** materials suitable for the different teaching and learning situations.

Below is a graph showing the division of hours by the sections established in SE Resolution 88/2007.

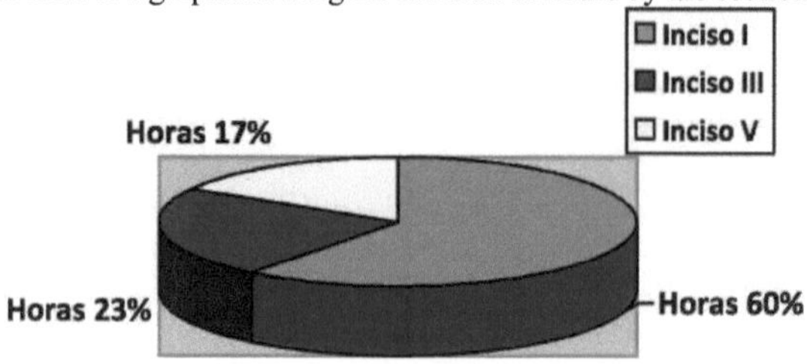

Graph 12 - Distribution of hours allocated to pedagogical activities, based on Art. 2 of SE No. 88/2007.

Out of a total of three hundred and eighty-five hours worked as a Coordinating Teacher, the group of eleven CPs used a total of one hundred and thirty-nine hours during the week in which the survey was carried out for the pedagogical activities proposed in SE Resolution 88/2007, contained in Article 2, in particular Items I, III and V. This represents 36.10 per cent of the workload established for this purpose.

The difference between the two hundred and forty-six hours worked was divided between other administrative and organisational activities, such as preparing meetings, meetings with managers, filling in spreadsheets and official documents, attending to parents, preparing events, monitoring disciplinary problems, helping the vice-principal with administrative issues, contacting the Guardianship Council, checking emails and replacing teachers. Some of the tasks carried out showed a real deviation from their duties, such as monitoring pupils leaving school, opening the school office, filling in secretarial documents, checking teachers' points, collecting medical certificates to compensate for absences, and studying legislation. When this calculation is finalised, we can see that this totals 63.89% of hours used.

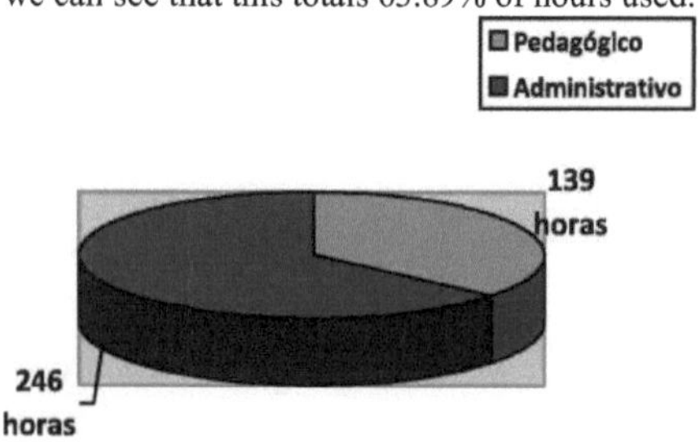

Graph 13: Distribution of hours worked - administrative versus pedagogical focus

CHAPTER 7

CONCLUSION

The Coordinating Teacher is undeniably an important component in the school organisation. They are at the centre of the teacher-student-school triad, which extends to other subjects directly or indirectly involved in this educational environment. It should therefore come as no surprise that there is a growing body of research into this professional and the environment that surrounds him or her. According to Placco, Laurinda and Souza (2011), in their presentation of the results of the research carried out by the Carlos Chagas Foundation on behalf of the Victor Civita Foundation, five hundred studies on the subject of "pedagogical coordination" were found in the Brazilian Digital Library of Theses and Dissertations (BDTD) from 1981 to 2010, of which around two hundred were related to the school context. The same procedure was carried out with the Bank of Theses and Dissertations of the Coordination for the Improvement of Higher Education Personnel / Ministry of Education (Capes/MEC), and this platform found, from 1987 to 2009, seventy-seven theses and four hundred and forty dissertations distributed among thirty-five universities.

The Teacher Coordinator theme is provocative because its constitution invokes different types of knowledge, distributed primarily between pedagogical and administrative competences. The set of skills, "knowing how to do" and "knowing how to be", are correlated in the work environment almost concomitantly and, as the interviewees' reports show, in an unbalanced way. They are challenged all the time to articulate this pedagogical, curricular, managerial and inter-relational knowledge, among others.

When the position of Teacher Coordinator was first created, its basic duties were already outlined in Decrees 5.586/75 and 7.709/76, and it was to be dedicated to the areas of planning, assistance, training and evaluation. All these duties were related to the teacher and the headteacher, but centred on improving the quality of teaching in the pedagogical field. For twenty years, the Coordinating Teacher held a position in the São Paulo State Education network. The crux of this study comes from the legislative changes of 1996, with Resolution 28/1996. The changes in the educational policy proposals of the State of São Paulo with regard to State Schools led to changes in the designations of the Coordinating Teacher, from the change in the nomenclature of the main occupation to the basic requirements for being hired to occupy the function, and no longer a position. For eleven years, different nomenclatures have been in place concurrently, with the Pedagogical

Coordinator being the civil servant who is still on active duty, and the 'new' Pedagogical Coordinator Teacher being elected to fulfil the role of coordinator. With SE Resolution 88/2007, the attributes and minimum qualification requirements to fulfil the role of Teacher Coordinator were legally declared.

The nervous point detected in the revised legislation is the change in the minimum academic qualification requirements for the position, as well as who will be responsible for assessing the selection process. Candidates for this position are no longer required to have a full degree in pedagogy, and will no longer be chosen by teachers from the school unit. They can have a degree in any area, and the decision on their choice will be made by the Teaching Supervisor of the Teaching Directorate and the Principal of the School Unit.

The literature review shows that the authors are concerned about the profile of the CP, who should present himself as a professional responsible for transforming and articulating the collective work of the school, one who stimulates reflection, creativity and innovation. However, in the interviews, they say that they are immersed in routine administrative activities that do not allow them to fulfil the role described above with the quality they desire.

Considering that the interviewees in this research are within the legal proposal of the 2007 Resolution, that they are aware of the transforming and articulating role of the PC, and the results obtained from analysing the research, it becomes possible to answer the questions raised in the objectives of this work.

In relation to the general objective of this study "To assess the performance of the Teacher Coordinator in the state public school system in the city of Mauá, in the state of São Paulo, in their day-to-day work, in terms of their functions and attributions, established by legislation", it was observed that the participants in this research carry out the tasks recommended in the sections of the legislation that governs them. Of the one hundred and thirty-nine hours worked on pedagogical tasks by the group of eleven PCs, 60 per cent of this amount is used to monitor and evaluate the teaching-learning process, as well as the results and performance of the students. The group of CPs used 23 per cent of their available time on continuing training for their peers. At this point in the research, there is a conflict in the literature reviews, whose authors insist and defend that the main role of the CP is the ongoing training of teachers, either in the school itself, in collective pedagogical work hours or individual assistance, or by encouraging participation in courses, congresses, seminars, technical orientations. The texts suggest that the coordinator's duties, with regard to the training dimension, are based on: promoting the coordination of the school team in order to draw up the school's political-pedagogical project; mediating interpersonal relations; planning, organising and conducting pedagogical meetings; dealing with the power relations unleashed in the school; carrying out his or her practice taking into account the diversity of teachers and schools; making written records as a way of sustaining the authorship of his or her role in the school. The revisions to the Resolutions that support the Coordinating Teacher and the Pedagogical Management Support Coordinating Teacher also emphasise these attributions. And finally, during the research, the participants in this study recorded that they carried out their duties in a standardised way, following the script in the School Management Handbook (2008).

As for the first specific objective, "To analyse the effectiveness and efficiency of the activities carried out by the Teacher Coordinator in relation to the duties laid down in the legislation", the PCs who took part use less than 50% of their working time to carry out activities laid down in the legislation. When you consider that effectiveness is about what you do, doing the right things, making the right choices, you can see from the answers to the questionnaires that the CPs interviewed are not satisfied with the amount of time they can devote to the duties laid down in the law, so they may not achieve the objectives of developing the continuing education they want during the proposed ATPCs, because there is a conflict of interest between what you have to do and what you have to do. One of the PCs interviewed clearly relates this feeling, saying that "In the two hours a week of HTPC, we have to divide the time between errands, training and organising the weekly schedule for the following week

Comparing the third and fourth specific objectives, "Identify the functions and attributions of the Teacher Coordinator in the performance and execution of tasks, in the act of action" and "Compare the legislation in force and the praxis of the Teacher Coordinator in the act of action", with the results taken from the Activity Log and the answers given in the interview script, we can see the different faces that the Teacher Coordinator incorporates during his working day. He carries out tasks within the scope established by the São Paulo State Department of Education, as described in the School Management Manual (2008), but he sees himself as being more involved in administrative management than pedagogy. The results of this study are in favour of the latter observation, as the group of PCs participating in this study spent 63.87% of their time carrying out administrative tasks. We can also see the literal deviation from the duties reported in the Activity Log when some of the informants state that they "check teachers' points", "validate sick leave certificates", "look after students when they leave", among other small activities that are the duty of the secretary or the student inspector.

The fifth specific objective, "To analyse which functions and attributions the Teacher Coordinator believes are due to his effective performance in the school", shows that all the pedagogical attributions are understood to be his. In analysing the answers to the interviews, the PCs emphasise the importance of the ATPC to carry out their role as teacher and student trainers, which is why they ask to have more time for this task. However, in the day-to-day running of the school, CPs take on other roles due to internal and external factors, whether emergency or routine, which they don't dispute - they simply absorb them.

At the end of the work, it is possible to understand that the questions raised in the work were answered due to the correct choice of the qualitative method supported by the data collection tools, as well as their analysis based on the specific theorists for each problem observed.

The general objective was answered by demonstrating that the Teacher Coordinators know what their roles are within the school and understand that they must dedicate themselves to teacher development because they are responsible for their ongoing training. However, they do not relate their duties directly to the Resolutions, since almost 50% of them are not familiar with their content. They find themselves stuck following a script already programmed by the bodies that manage them, a statement that is borne out by looking at the almost identical records of the CPs' daily activities. It's clear that the time they use for teacher development is scarce, or in most cases, poorly utilised - as evidenced by the distribution of tasks in this research.

The specific objectives were met because they demonstrate the difficulty of distributing tasks and fulfilling assignments, and therefore run counter to the proposal set out in the legislation that supports the Teacher Coordinator. Many of the CPs carry out the tasks requested of them, but are unable to measure results. There is always a feeling in the interviewees' speeches that they don't have enough time to carry out the tasks they consider important.

In concluding this research, aware of the limitations of academic and scientific studies, it can be said that the work does not end in itself, or in the results of the analyses found here. It is hoped that it has helped to expand this theme and field of study. The topic is indeed important and should be continued by adopting quantitative methods, thus expanding the number of respondents in other municipalities and, consequently, expanding the results for their next validations.

7.1 PROPOSALS AND RECOMMENDATIONS

A quick look at the work scenario of the CP reveals that, during the course of this study, it was clear that educational policy reforms and changes in legislation have modified the role of the Teacher Coordinator in the school environment. As a result, this professional's power of "authority" has been weakened and, on the other hand, their training is not as favoured in higher education or pedagogy courses.

The São Paulo State Department of Education, concerned about instrumentalising the Teacher Coordinator, has created the School Management Booklet, which describes step by step the actions that he will have to carry out during his job. They are responsible for announcing, monitoring and implementing the São Paulo State Department of Education's Curriculum Proposal, which is why they have to develop, as well as communication skills, a political and pedagogical stance that is open to dialogue, collaborative and transparent.

The last specific objective presented in the work, "To propose guidelines for the functions and attributions of the Teacher Coordinator, taking into account current legislation, school praxis and the understanding of due performance in the act of action, seeking to make the role of the PC legitimate, as a manager with the teachers in the school", is linked to the problem that the work of the Teacher Coordinator is a multidetermined know-how.

This professional ends up developing other skills, usually with a large administrative input, which end up being honed and adjusted to the school environment in an induced way, and without formal learning.

The purpose of this work is to think about equipping the Teacher Coordinator with academic training focused on the attributions and profile desired by the professional who will occupy the position of PC, based on SE Resolutions No. 88/2007 and SE No. 3/2013.

These include the following competences:

-planning;

-monitoring, and;

-evaluate.

Pursuing the attributes of:

-dynamism;

-leadership;

- interpersonal relationships;

- teamwork;

- notions of democratic and participatory management, and;

- proactive attitudes with collaborative action.

Therefore, as a complement to the ongoing work of continuing education focussed on pedagogical management for this professional, it is important to rethink training at higher education level, suggesting an academic curriculum in which all degree courses have specific subjects in administrative management training for Teacher Coordinators. This action could equip the future Teacher Coordinator and adapt them to the new requirements of educational institutions in the state of São Paulo, which, through the evolution of their Resolutions, aim to hire a professional pedagogue with a strongly structured and qualified profile as an educational manager.

REFERENCES

ALARCÃO, Isabel; TAVARES, José. **Supervisão da prática pedagógica**: uma perspectiva de desenvolvimento e aprendizagem. 2. ed. rev. e actualiz. Coimbra: Ed. Almedina, 2010.

ALMEIDA, Laurinha Ramalho de; PLACCO, Vera Maria Nigro de Souza (org.) **O coordenador pedagógico e as questões de contemporaneidade**. São Paulo: Loyola, 2011.

ALVAREZ, Maria Esmeralda Ballestero. **Organisation, systems and methods**. São Paulo: McGraw Hill, 1990. v. 2.

ANDREUCCI, S. B. **O coordenador pedagógico na rede oficial de ensino em São Paulo**: relato de uma experiência em alfabetização. São Paulo, 1989. Master's dissertation. School of Psychology, Pontifical Catholic University, São Paulo, 1989.

ARAÚJO, Sâmara Carla Lopes Guerra. **Being a pedagogical coordinator teacher**: about teaching work and autonomy, 2007. Master's dissertation. Postgraduate Programme in Education, Federal University of Minas Gerais. Belo Horizonte, 2007.

BARDIN, Laurence. **Content analysis**. Lisbon, Portugal: Edições 70, 1977.

BARROSO, João et al. The internal regulation of schools: logics and actors. In: BARROSO, João (Org.) **A regulação das políticas públicas de educação**: espaços, dinâmicas e actores. Lisbon: Educa, 2006. p. 163-190.

BALLESTERO ALVAREZ, Maria Esmeralda. **Organisation, systems and methods**. São Paulo: Ed. Macgraw Hill, 1991. v.2.

BRAZIL, LAW No. 9.394 GUIDELINES AND BASES FOR NATIONAL EDUCATION. Promulgated on 20 December 1996. Abrelivros Associação Brasileira dos Editores de Livros, 1996.

BRUNO, Eliane Bambini Gorgueira; ALMEIDA, Laurinha Ramalho de; CHRISTOV, Luiza Helena da Silva (org.) **O coordenador pedagógico e a formação docente**. São Paulo: Loyola, 2009.

BRUNO, Eliane Bambini Gorgueira; CHRISTOV, Luiza Helena da Silva (org.) **O coordenador pedagógico e a educação continuada**. São Paulo: Loyola, 2009.

CELESTINO, Marcos Roberto. **Pedagogical Coordination and the teaching staff**: the importance of continuing training. **Revista Acadêmica**, n.9, p. 31-44, jan./jun. 2012.

CHIAVENATO, I. **Teoria geral da administração**. 5. ed. São Paulo: Makron Books, 1997.

CHRISTOV, Luiza Helena da Silva. **Intentions and problems in pedagogical coordination practices**. São Paulo: Loyola, 2010.

CLEMENTI, N. The voice of others and our voice. In: ALMEIDA, L. R.; PLACCO, V. M. N. **O Coordenador pedagógico e o espaço da mudança.** São Paulo: Loyola, 2001. p. 53-66.

COSTA, Maria Emília (coord.). **Conflict management at school**. Lisbon: Universidade Aberta, 2003.

CHRISTOV, L. H. S. **The pedagogical coordinator's knowledge:** interpersonal entanglements and (con)sciences at school. 2001. 162 f. Thesis (Doctorate in Educational Psychology) Pontifical Catholic University, São Paulo, 2001.

CUNHA, Renata C. O. Barirchelo; PRADO, Guilherme do Val Toledo. **Teachers and their training**: representations of pedagogical coordinators, 2006. **Gest. Ação**, Salvador, v.9, n.3, p. 381-392, Sep./Dec. 2006.

DEMO, Pedro. **Pesquisa e construção do conhecimento**: metodologia científica no caminho de Habermas. Rio de Janeiro: Tempo Brasileiro, 1994.

DIAS-DA-SILVA, M. H. G. F.; LOURENCETTI. G. C. A Voz dos professores e algumas reformas educacionais nas séries finais do ensino fundamental: desenvolvimento ou impasse? In: SAMPAIO, M. M. F. **O cotidiano escolar face às políticas educacionais.** Araraquara: JM, 2002. p. 21-43.

DOMINGUES, Isaneida. **The pedagogical coordinator and the challenge of continuous teacher training at school**. 2009, 235p. Thesis (Doctorate) Postgraduate Programme in Education. Faculty of Education, University of São Paulo. São Paulo, 2009.

ELIAS, M. del C. **A questão da autoridade no desempenho da função da coordenação pedagógica.** São Paulo, 1983. Master's dissertation. Faculty of Education, Pontifical Catholic University, São Paulo, 1983.

FERNANDES, Maria José da Silva. The pedagogical coordinator teacher in São Paulo state schools: from pedagogical articulation to the management of educational reforms. **Educação e Pesquisa**, São Paulo, v. 38, n. 04, p. 799-814, Oct./Dec. 2012.

_____. Pedagogical coordination in São Paulo state schools: recent resolutions and daily updating in the management of school organisation. **RBPAE**, v.27, n.3, p. 361-588, sep./dec. 2011.

_____. The pedagogical coordinator teacher and the fragility of the career. **Estudos em Avaliação Educacional,** v. 20, n. 44, p. 411- 424, Sep/Dec. 2009.

_____. **Problematising the work of the pedagogical coordinator teacher in São Paulo state public schools**. 2004. 113f. Dissertation (Master's in School Education) Faculty of Sciences and Letters, São Paulo State University, Araraquara, 2004. Available at: www.biblioteca.unesp.br/bibliotecadigital/document/?did=3415. Accessed on: 14 August 2012.

_____. **The pedagogical coordinator teacher, the articulation of the collective and teaching working conditions in São Paulo state public schools. After all, what's left of this role?** Available at: www.anpae.org.br/congressos antigos/simposio2007/302.pdf Accessed on: 14 Aug. 2012.

FERREIRA, Naura Syria Carapeto. **Supervisão educacional:** uma reflexão crítica. 13. ed. Petrópolis: Vozes, 2007.

FRANCO, Denise Vieira. **Pedagogical coordinator**: identity in question, 2006. Dissertation (Master's Degree) - Postgraduate Programme in Education - Federal University of Juiz de Fora, MG. Juiz de Fora, 2006. 190 p.

FREIRE, Paulo. **A pedagogia da autonomia**: saberes necessárias à prática educativa. Rio de Janeiro: EGA, 1996.

_____. Education: a possible dream. In: BRANDÃO, Carlos R. (org.). **O educador**: vida e morte. 2. ed. Rio de Janeiro: Graal, 1982.

VICTOR CIVITA FOUNDATION. **The pedagogical coordinator and teacher training**: intentions, tensions and contradictions. 2011. Available at: www.fvc.org.br/.../Relatório%20Fmal%20Coordenadores%20Pedagogic... Accessed on: 23 December 2013.

_____. **Continuing teacher education in Brazil**: an analysis of modalities and practices, commissioned by the Victor Civita Foundation. 2011. Available at: www.fvc.org.br/pdf/relatorio-formacao-continuada.pdf Accessed on: 23 Dec. 2013.

GARCIA, M. **Coordenação pedagógica**: ação, interação, trans-formação. São Paulo. 1995. Master's dissertation. Faculty of Education, Pontifical Catholic University, São Paulo, 1995.

GATTI, B. A.; BERNARDES, N. M. G.; MELLO, G. N. de. Study on the role of the teaching assistant. **Cadernos de Pesquisa**, n. 9, p. 4-40. Mar. 1974.

GIL, Antônio Carlos. **Methods and techniques of social research**. São Paulo: Atlas, 1999.

GODOY, Arilda S. **Introduction to qualitative research and its possibilities**. In: Revista de Administração de Empresas, v. 35, n.2, Mar./Apr. 1995, p. 57-63.

JUSBRASIL. http://www.jusbrasil.com.br/legislacao/anotada/3762179/art-2-do-decreto- 5586-75-sao-paulo. Accessed: 26/01/13.

LAKATOS, E. M.; MARCONI, M. de A. **Metodologia científica**. São Paulo: Atlas, 1995.

LIMA, Licinio Lima. **The school as an educational organisation**: a sociological approach. São Paulo: Cortez, 2001.

LOMONICO, Circe Ferreira. **Atribuições do coordenador pedagógico**. 3. ed. São Paulo. Edicon, 2005.

_____. **Coordenador Pedagógico**: o técnico e psicopedagogo institucional. 3. ed. São Paulo. Edicon, 2005.

_____. **Evaluation of the performance of the Pedagogical Coordinator's update in underprivileged schools in the metropolitan region of São Paulo**, 1980. Dissertation (Master's Degree) - Educational Psychology Programme - Pontifical Catholic University of São Paulo, São Paulo, 1980.

LIMA, Paulo Gomes; SANTOS, Sandra Mendes de. The pedagogical coordinator in basic education: challenges and perspectives. **Revista de Educação,** v. 2, n. 4, jul./dez. 2007, p.77-90.

LIMA, Elma Corrêa de. A historical look at supervision, in. RANGEL, Mary (org.). **Supervisão pedagógica:** princípios e práticas. 8. ed. Campinas, SP: Papirus. 2008, p. 69-80.

LUCK, Heloísa. **Ação integrada**: administração, supervisão e orientação educacional. 28. ed. Petrópolis, RJ: Vozes, 2011.

MAGALHÃES, Poliana Marina Mascarenhas de Santana. **Teachers listening to the pedagogical coordinator's know-how:** a study in social representation. In:

INTERNATIONAL COLLOQUIUM "EDUCATION AND CONTEMPORANEITY", 5, 2011. **Proceedings...**São Cristovão-SE, 2011. Available at: www.educonufs.com.br/vcoloquiointernacional. Accessed on: 07 March 2013.

MATTAR, F. N. **Pesquisa de marketing**: metodologia e planejamento. 5. ed. São Paulo: Atlas, 1999. v. 1.

MATE, C. H. What is the identity of the pedagogical coordinator teacher? In: GUIMARÃES, A. A. et al. **O Coordenador pedagógico e a educação continuada**. São Paulo: Loyola, 2010. p. 19-23.

MINTZBERG, Henry. **The manager's Job:** Folklore and Fact. New Jersey: Prentice-Hall 1978.

MINAYO, M. C. S. (Org.). **Pesquisa social**: teoria, método e criatividade. Petrópolis: Vozes, 2001.

MURRIE, Zuleika de Felice. **Caderno do gestor:** gestão **do** currículo na escola. São Paulo: SEE,

2008. v. 1.

NEVES, José Luís. Qualitative research: characteristics, uses and possibilities. **Caderno de Pesquisa em Administração**, São Paulo, v. 1, n. 3, p. 1-5, 2. sem./1996.

NEW SCHOOL: SCHOOL MANAGEMENT. The paths of pedagogical coordination and teacher training. Special Ed. N. 6, June 2011. Available at: https://www.google.com.br/#q=Gisela+Wajskop+... Accessed on: 10 October 2012.

NOVAES, Elaine Zipoli Martinez. **The pedagogical coordinator in public schools in the municipal network of Santos/SP**: contributions to assessment issues at primary school level. 2008, 198p. Dissertation (Master's Degree) Postgraduate Programme in Education - Catholic University of Santos, Santos, SP, 2008.

NÓVOA, Antônio. Teacher training and teacher education. In: Nóvoa, Antônio (org.) **Os professores e sua formação**. Lisbon: Dom Quixote, 1992.

OLIVEIRA, Jane Cordeiro de. **The power relations between the pedagogical coordinator, teachers and school headmaster:** some considerations. 2009. Available at: www.anpae.org.br/.../Trabalhos/JaneCordeiroOliveira res int GT8.pdf Accessed on: 23 Dec. 2013.

PARO, Vitor Henrique. Critique of the school structure. São Paulo: Cortez, 2011.

_____. **School administration**: a critical introduction. 17. ed. rev. and expanded. São Paulo: Cortez, 2012.

PLACCO, Vera Maria Nigro de Souza. The pedagogical coordinator in the confrontation with everyday school life. In: PLACCO, Vera Maria Nigro de Souza; ALMEIDA, Laurinda Ramalho de (org.) **O coordenador pedagógico e o cotidiano da escola**. São Paulo: Loyola, 2010. p. 44-60.

_____. **Challenges for the pedagogical coordinator in collective school work**: intervention or prevention? São Paulo: Loyola, 2010.128 p.

PLACCO, Vera Maria Nigro de Souza; ALMEIDA, Laurinda Ramalho de (org.) **O coordenador pedagógico e o atendimento à diversidade**. São Paulo: Loyola, 2010.

PLACCO, Vera Maria Nigro de Souza; SOUZA, Vera Lucia Trevisan de; ALMEIDA, Laurinda Ramalho de. **The pedagogical coordinator: contributions to proposing public policies**. Caderno de Pesquisa, v. 42, n. 147, p. 754-771, Sep./Dec. 2012.

ROMAN, Marcelo Domingues. **The pedagogical coordinator teacher and everyday school life**: an ethnographic study. São Paulo, 2001. Dissertation (Master's Degree) Institute of Psychology, University of São Paulo. São Paulo, 2001.

RUSSO, Miguel Henrique. Schools and management paradigms. **ECCOS - Rev. Cient., UNINOVE**, São Paulo, v. 6, n. 1, p.25-42. 2004.

_____. Work and school administration: development and appropriation of the meaning they assume in the pedagogical production process, 2011. **RBPAE** - v.27, n.3, p. 361-588, Sep/Dec 2011.

_____. **Contributions of the General Theory of Administration to the understanding of school organisation and management**. 2012. Version 4. author's own Feb 2012.

RUSSO, Miguel Henrique; CARVALHO, Celso. **Reform and education policies of the São Paulo state government (2007-2011).** Available at: www.anpae.org.br/iberoamericano2012/.../MiguelRusso res int GT7.pdf Accessed on: 15 Dec. 2013.

SALVADOR, Cristina Maria. **Pedagogical coordination: a rereading based on Paulo Freire.** Available at: www.paulofreire.ufpb.br/paulofreire/Files/seminarios/mesa02-b.pdf. Accessed on: 10 Feb. 2013.

SÃO PAULO, SECRETARIA DO ESTADO DE SÃO PAULO. Legislation for the coordinating teacher. Available at: http://www.educacao.sp.gov.br/lise/sislegis/pesqpalchav.asp?assunto=145. Accessed on: 08 June 2012.

SEVERINO, Antonio Joaquim. **Metodologia do trabalho científico**. 22. ed. rev. e ampl. São Paulo: Cortez, 2002.

SILVA, Adalberto. **The role of the pedagogical coordinator in teacher training**. 2012, 127p. Dissertation (Master's Degree) Postgraduate Programme in Education - Methodist University of the State of São Paulo - UMESP. São Paulo, 2012.

SILVEIRA, Amélia. et al. **Roteiro básico para apresentação e editoração de teses, dissertações e monografias**. 3. ed. Blumenau: Edifurb, 2009.

SIMCSIK, Tímbor. **Organisation, systems and methods**. São Paulo: Futura, 2001.

THEODORSON, G. A.; THEODORSON, A. G. A **modern dictionary of sociology**. London, Methuen, 1970.

TRIVINOS, A. N. S. **Introdução à pesquisa em ciências sociais**: a pesquisa qualitativa em educação. São Paulo: Atlas, 1987.

VIEIRA, Marili M. da Silva. The pedagogical coordinator and the feelings involved in everyday life. In: PLACCO, V. M. N. de S.; ALMEIDA, L. R. de. (org.). **O coordenador pedagógico e o cotidiano da escola**. São Paulo: Edições Loyola, 2010. p. 83-92

WALTRICK, Rose Elaine de Liz. **The pedagogical coordinator in early childhood education in the municipal education network of Florianópolis**: marks of a democratic experience. 2008, 178p. Dissertation (Master's Degree) Postgraduate Programme in Education - Federal University of Santa Catarina, Florianópolis, 2008.

WALDMANN Ivanete Menegon; SCHNELTZLER, Roseli P. **Professor coordenador pedagógico e formação docente continuada**. Methodist University of Piracicaba, Postgraduate Programme in

Education - Teaching profession and training of educators - Communication, SP (n.d.).

MIX
Papier aus verantwortungsvollen Quellen
Paper from responsible sources
FSC® C105338

Printed by Books on Demand GmbH, Norderstedt / Germany